D1612835

Books should be returned on or before the
last date stamped below.

64

-5. MAY 1977

10. JUN. 1977

28. JUL. 1977

18. NOV. 1977
-2. AUG. 1978
28. APR. 1979

27. JUN. 1979
-5. NOV. 1979

12. NOV. 1980

16. NOV. 1987

-9. JAN. 1984

ABERDEENSHIRE
LIBRARY &
INFORMATION SERVICES
ABERDEENSHIRE
25 JUN 1992
WITHDRAWN
INFORMATIONSERV.N
FROM LIBRARY
WITH
FROM

NORTH EAST of SCOTLAND LIBRARY SERVICE
14 Crown Terrace, Aberdeen

MCLAUGHLIN, W.R.D.

Call to the south

6.   AT39

CALL TO THE SOUTH

By the same author
ANTARCTIC RAIDER

Call to the South

*A Story of British Whaling
in Antarctica*

W. R. D. McLaughlin

WHITE LION PUBLISHERS LIMITED
London, Sydney and Toronto

To all Whalemen
Whatever their Nationality
who answer
The Call of the South

First published in Great Britain 1962
by George Harrap & Co.Ltd.

Copyright © W.R.D. McLaughlin 1962

White Lion Edition 1976

ISBN 7274 0114 9

Made and printed in Great Britain
for White Lion Publishers Limited,
138 Park Lane, London W1Y 3DD
by Hendington Limited,
Lion House, North Town, Aldershot, Hampshire

AT39
6.

969767

Preface

APELAGIC, or seaborne, whaling expedition in Antarctica consists of a large factory ship attended by about a dozen fast catcher vessels and a number of other craft used for towing in dead whales. British expeditions employ upward of six hundred men, most of them Scots and Norwegians.

When they have sailed across the world and reached the Far South the whale-catching season lasts for only ten to twelve weeks. During this frenzy of intense effort work goes on twenty-four hours a day in all weathers, but always in intense cold. And in this brief time anything from two thousand to two thousand five hundred whales are hunted and killed by the catcher vessels and delivered up to the factory ship for processing into oil and by-products.

This book is an account of a typical British expedition to Antarctica. It describes every aspect of modern scientific whaling, and tells of the men who serve in whaling ships, whose work is so little known to the rest of the world. The romance may have gone out of modern whaling, but the adventure and excitement are still there. Whaling is now a streamlined, highly mechanized industry, and most of the men in it are skilled specialists. The old dangers of the open boat and hand-harpoon encounters with the whale have long since gone, but many new dangers and hazards have been added, as you shall hear.

But no book on whaling can ignore the grave threat of extinction which hangs over the most majestic of warm-blooded animals. The increasing wholesale slaughter of whales puts in peril the continued existence of the great baleens and of the whaling industry itself.

During the 1960–61 season twenty-one expeditions operated in the Antarctic, and the number of whales killed at sea was 38,812. The production of baleen- and sperm-oil amounted to 2,146,472 barrels (six barrels to the ton). In addition, during the 1960–61 season Antarctic land stations at South Georgia killed 2317 whales.

International regulations have failed to avert the danger that the giant oil-producing whales will be exterminated by man's greed for profit. So this is also a plea by a whaling man who has spent many seasons in Antarctica for action to save the whale before it is too late.

Now, come whaling with me, and you shall judge the facts for yourself. Let me introduce you to the tough men who hunt the whale. You shall see them at work in fair weather and foul. And you shall witness the strange wonders of those Southern waters, the loneliest places in the world.

W.R.D.M.

At sea, July 1962

Contents

Illustrations

*The photographs reproduced in this book were taken by R. (Bob) Squires,
C. K. Crockett, O.B.E., M.M., and J. H. Brown.*

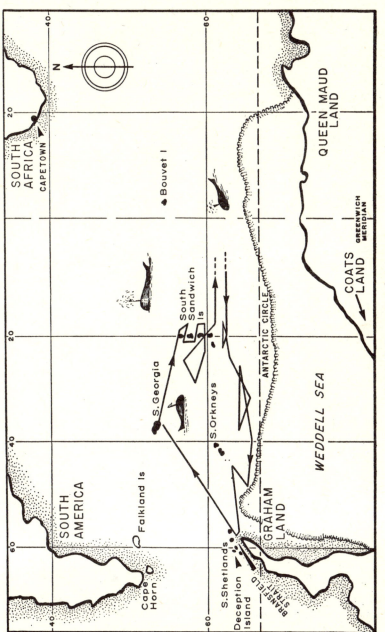

Typical Operational Area

I

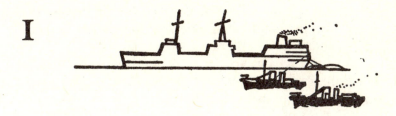

The defenceless monster

SUMMER in the frozen continent of Antarctica is from November to April, and as warmth unlocks the grip of ice along its mountainous coasts, the fringes begin to crack and crumble. The glaciers and piled cliffs of ice break into bergs and then into pack-ice and floes. In this white world the huge baleen whales are lords of creation.

The whales thrash their way southward from the tropic zones for the Antarctic summer, when for many weeks there is no darkness. The biggest of the baleens in this monstrous migration may be as heavy as a whole herd of elephants. His heart alone may weigh 1000 pounds. And he is desperately hungry when he arrives.

From May to October the whales bask in the warm seas to the north, entirely concerned with mating and family life. They eat nothing in all these months. But the honeymoon ends, the giant babies are strong enough to travel, and the procession of whales churns steadily to the feeding-grounds. The seas of Antarctica are heavily stocked with minute shrimp-like life called krill or plankton, a rich diet on which the whales soon grow fat. It extends from the surface to a depth of fifty fathoms. Surging ahead with open jaws, the whales can take in a ton of this food at a gulp. They feed day and night.

But as the whales go south, so does man, the hunter. This is man's chance in a short season of slaughter to gather one of the most profitable harvests in the world. Every year millions of pounds are spent on elaborate expeditions fitted with every scientific device to hunt and kill the whale. Every year millions of pounds of profit are made in this gory trade.

The oil of the whale has become an essential part of the food supply of modern man. In a world where want or semi-starvation haunts two-thirds of the human race whale-oil plays an important part in nutrition.

But in the battle of man versus whale, man's part is not worthy of his superior intelligence. The commercial interests of many nations which have poured capital into whale-hunting in a race for profits have wantonly over-exploited the rich resources of Antarctica for many years. Nobody knows this better than the men who take part in modern whaling. No whaling man is made so callous or so self-centred by the bitter cold, the grinding work, and the overwhelming loneliness of Antarctica that he cannot spare a pang of pity and remorse for his prey, the whale.

The death of this defenceless mammal in all its horror is, in fact, a load on the minds of many whaling men, even when they have spent a lifetime at the work. But, on the other hand, man is a hunter and an adventurer. His long, atavistic memory makes him glory in the chase and the kill. Moreover, he is driven by strong economic forces to leave his home waters, where for the sailor a living may be poor and uncertain, and to seek the rewards and challenges of a whaler's life.

Man is a killer, but a killer with a conscience. This is the strange paradox of man versus whale. This is the struggle of mind and body which possesses the whaleman in one of the most strenuous and dangerous jobs on earth. This is why the whalemen curses his hard life, but goes back to Antarctica year after year. This is why I tell, not only of the thrill of the chase, the wild excitement of the kill, but also the grim facts of the whale's fight for life and his inevitable, cruel death.

The death of the bull on the sword of the matador— *Death in the Afternoon*, Ernest Hemingway called it—has fascinated and repelled men for centuries. It is a ritualistic and symbolic drama in which man plays out his own inevitable mortality. The death of the whale was described more than a hundred years ago with the same symbolic and ritualistic significance by Herman Melville. But there is no longer any comparison between Melville's highly imaginative saga of Moby Dick in the eighteen-fifties and the scientific slaughter of whales in the nineteen-sixties. The whale is no longer a worthy protagonist of man; nor can his struggle for life be presented as a grand tragedy. It is a sordid hunt. The whale has become the helpless victim of the floating *abattoir*. His death can no longer be romanticized.

The introduction of the helicopter for spotting whales from the air took away the last sporting chance of escape that the whale had. Aircraft had been tried before, but with little or no success. But the helicopter has great advantages: it requires little stowage space and can land and take off in small, confined areas; it can spot, follow, and hover over its intended victim like a great vulture; it can call up a whaleboat by radio-telephone and then wait for the hunters to come plunging through the seas; it can advise the whale-shooter throughout the final stages of the kill because the mammal's underwater movements can be seen from above.

One whaling firm tried out the helicopter. Others, fearing that the innovation would give this expedition an unfair advantage, immediately followed suit. Conversion was simple. Small, steel flight decks were built up high in the superstructures, and the modern whaleship now carries at least two helicopters. The waters of Antarctica are constantly patrolled by these yellow- and black-striped aircraft in their frantic search for whales. Mortality among pilots has been high, but there is no dearth of competent airmen.

The use of the helicopter has meant that a constant plot can now be kept of the ice conditions to the southward. Within the ice-packs there are large tracts of open water where whales are sometimes abundant. Modern whale-gunners without the aid of helicopters are chary of entering this ice in search of whales. Time means money, and any delay in getting through the heavy pack cancels all that may be gained. Now the whaleboats can penetrate the ice edge with every confidence, knowing that they will be warned if the ice shows signs of closing in around them and making the passage outward difficult.

The helicopters, or 'choppers,' are an integral part of any pelagic expedition. They proved their usefulness from the start, not only in their main function of searching for the whale. They also saved lives by their rapid mobility in taking injured seamen from whaleboat to factory ship for medical care. Many other types of work have come easily to these craft and their intrepid pilots, who face extreme risks. In waters the most dangerous in the world sudden squalls of almost hurricane force can spring up without warning. Fog is prevalent and can sometimes last for days. To be caught away from the parent ship at such times is very perilous, and valuable lives have been lost.

For all the bravery of the pilots and their help in the hunt, old whalemen were aghast at the introduction of the helicopter. "Searching for whales from the air!" one old worthy exclaimed sadly. "Where the hell is it all going to end? They'll be shooting the ruddy things from the air next."

Indeed, whaling has reached such a peak of efficiency that nothing short of killing from the air would make the modern whaleman raise a quizzical eyebrow. Perhaps it could be done—some form of missile with a compressed-air explosive head which could force air into the blood-stream and kill the mammals, and at the same time keep them afloat. Many experiments have been made with the idea of electrocuting the whale, and this may soon be an everyday method—if there are enough whales left to make the hunt worth while. For all these modern inventions and the paraphernalia of equipment will not repopulate the waters with whales.

"Scientific whaling? Bah, that's not the trouble with the whaling industry to-day," scoffed one of our older British hands. "It's big business that has ruined the whaling racket. They're all too damned greedy. They want too much profit."

This whaleman was an ardent preacher against the indiscriminate killing of baleen whales. That he had made a living by this killing for nearly thirty years didn't deter him. He still aimed his views at all who would listen.

There is another school of thought more concerned with the cruel way the whale dies than with the number of whales killed. And these reformers certainly have a case. There is no doubt that the animal suffers. How few people realize the cruelty, the brutality, that is involved in chasing, harpooning, and killing the whale. How few people realize the despairing fight it puts up before dying of convulsions with an explosive shrapnel grenade tearing at its vitals. It has to be seen to be believed.

The whale certainly knows it is being hunted. It reacts with obvious panic to the sight of a ship. It probably knows it will be killed if it can't get away from the powerful throb of the ship's propellers. It sounds, and stays submerged for as long as possible before it is compelled to surface in order to breathe. The catcher vessel and its screw are still there, watching remorselessly. The whale has to surface at more frequent intervals. The whale-gunner gets closer. He is within range. He sights and presses the trigger.

The first harpoon rarely kills. Two, three, up to six, harpoons have to be used before some animals die. The whaleboat lies to a taut line, the whale nearly a mile away, somewhere out ahead still fighting, pulling with a force as powerful as a locomotive. As it tries to dislodge the harpoon from its body it tears itself to pieces. Slowly it dies a cruel death.

2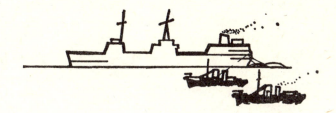

The harpoon strikes home

IN my job as senior deck executive officer of a modern whale-factory ship it was not often that I got the chance to go whale-hunting. But when I did I was right there. In spite of what I have said about the death of the whale I found the chase irresistibly exciting.

So come with me on number two whaleboat as she lies refuelling alongside the mother ship. Let's see what happens in a typical day of whale-hunting with the gunner and his crew.

I stand on the gently swaying platform which is used as the fuelling-point, looking down at the small catcher vessel pitching and rolling below, but feel no qualms of uneasiness. I have done this many times before.

I seat myself in a large, circular basket, and, without any formality or warning, I am whipped high in the air by the aid of winch and derrick, and lowered to the deck of the

whaleboat as easily as descending to the ground floor of
an office building by electric lift. I scramble to my feet and
watch the crew cast off the moorings. The engines roar to
life, and we speed off to the distant horizon. One seaman
climbs to the look-out barrel. The whale-hunt is on . . . .

I have entered an entirely different world from the one
I have just left—a world of upheaving deck, of powerful
engines, and of clean, fresh air—a vast difference from the
slaughterhouse smells of the factory ship.

I climb to the bridge. The catcher vessel looks squat and
formidable, a ship to inspire confidence. Forward at the
bow the harpoon gun is loaded and ready for instant use.
The lethal barbed harpoon, with its pointed grenade
attachment, fused to explode three seconds after impact,
requires only finger compression to send it flying on its
mission of death. The nylon forelines, coiled with infinite
care at the bow leads, are rove through a system of spring-
tensioned blocks leading directly to a massive steam
hauling winch.

I peer over the front of the bridge. We are steering
towards a distant white glow which shows just above the
horizon—the blink from the ice edge of Antarctica. The
Norwegian whale-gunner is gazing through powerful pris-
matics. He turns and gives me a smile of welcome. "I
think we shall go into the ice to-day. We'll try for the blue
whales," he says. I look at the compass. We are steering
south-westerly. Around us in almost every direction are
the Southern Ocean icebergs. We pass one close to starboard—a menacing and frightening mountain of translucent, blue-white ice. Flat-topped, about two miles long
on one side, it is a typical barrier berg, broken off from a
glacier.

Now we enter a maze of tortuous channels that lead
through the ice-pack. Groups of elephant seals lie basking
on the ice-floes. They look up at us with seeming contempt,

aggressively, as if disputing the right of mere man to invade their domain. A solitary penguin waddles along close besides us, a lonely and pathetic figure in his black-and-white coat, and with red webbed feet.

We have just emerged into open water again when there is a loud hail from the look-out barrel. "Whale-*blast!* Starboard bow!"

Eyes swing to starboard. There, about three miles away, two feathery *blasts* can be seen rising into the air at frequent intervals. They hang momentarily before merging into the atmosphere.

The whale-gunner signals for full speed. The engines respond. "Blue whales," he yells exultantly. We are hunting the biggest whales of them all.

'*Blast*,' by the way, is the Norwegian word for 'blow,' and it is generally used in Antarctica. From a glance at the blow an experienced whale-gunner, the man who is in charge of a catcher ship, can tell almost with certainty the type of whale he is chasing and how big it is, to a foot or so. Many landsmen still think the whale blows out a jet of water: this was the belief for thousands of years from the days of ancient Greece. But the whaleman knows better. No jet of water would remain in the air for three to five seconds. The blow is a small cloud of vapour which the whale forces out of his blow-hole or -holes as he surfaces. It comes out under great pressure, and that is probably why it condenses and hangs in the air for several seconds before dispersing. Nobody is quite sure what this vapour consists of to make it visible from so far, but it is lucky for the hunter that it is so visible, for without it we should rarely catch the whale. The mammals must come to the surface to breathe, and so they betray their presence to man.

As we close with them I see the whale-gunner jumping about the gun platform, sometimes breaking into oaths,

and frantically waving his arms as he issues orders. I wait
with that unfailing excitement of expectation.

B-O-O-M! The gun roars. The harpoon hurls through
the air, and the whale-line follows. There is a momentary
silence, and then a muffled explosion as the time fuse
functions and fragments the grenade. The whale is thrash-
ing the water about a hundred feet off our starboard bow.

"Full astern," the gunner orders. "Slack away."

The whale-line begins to run from the line locker, at
first slowly, and then with a wild rush. The whale has
sounded.

There is now a fight between the mammal and the crew
of the catcher vessel—a fight to the death. It is a struggle
that can have only one result. Three-quarters of a mile of
whale-line has been slacked away when the gunner calls
a halt. The blue whale is fighting madly on the end of a
taut line—a line held by 500 tons of steel and powerful
engines. Even the vast strength of the whale cannot com-
pete with man's power. A 90-foot blue whale weighing 100
tons will cruise at fourteen to fifteen knots and, when
harpooned, will make fantastic, agonized bursts up to
twenty knots. It has been calculated that it develops the
equivalent of 500 horsepower in these bursts. The somewhat smaller fin whale does about ten to twelve knots in
normal cruising and has a top speed of sixteen to eighteen
knots when trying to escape from its pursuers.

The blue whale we have shot is tiring. Deep in its vast
body is the mortal wound, and even if it could shake off
the harpoon it would be doomed. Slowly but surely the
line is hove in. The ship's engines pull hard astern. The
gunner waits calmly now by the gun. He has loaded a
second harpoon with its lethal attachments. As the whale
is hauled back into range close under the bows the gun
booms again, and a second harpoon buries itself just behind
the dorsal fin, a little behind the enormous, arching back.

There is another dull explosion in the whale's vitals. Then come a series of convulsions—a last, despairing struggle. The whale spouts blood, keels slowly over, and floats belly upward. It is dead.

I watch the crew go to work on the carcass. It is quickly hauled alongside, and compressed air is blown into the stomach to keep it afloat. A small cork buoy is made fast in order to facilitate the work of the picking-up vessel, which will tow the cadaver back to the factory ship. Finally, a red flag, attached to a spear and bearing the whaleboat's number for all to see, is plunged into the blubber to prove that it belongs to that particular vessel.

While all this is being done by the crew the gunner is anxiously scanning the horizon for the other whale we spotted. Although it cannot now be seen, its exact bearings have been noted, and, within minutes of cutting the first cadaver adrift, we are speeding in that direction. We soon come up with it. The whale is wary. Every time it sounds it comes up again in a different direction, sometimes abeam, sometimes far astern. The gunner tries his best to scare it into running in one direction, but he fails. The whale is making for the ice-pack. We follow.

Now begins a chase that is to last three hours; a chase that ends nearly thirty miles from where it started; a wild chase that takes us through the most hazardous of broken-up ice-packs.

The whale can delay the finale, but it has no chance For three hours it tries desperately to elude its pursuers. Slowly the majestic animal tires. It sounds much more frequently and for shorter periods. The whaleboat's constant speed of fourteen knots is the deciding factor. The gunner waits patiently for his chance—and he takes it.

This second whale proves to be a female even more gigantic than the male we killed. What does it matter to the huge business interests we serve that these creatures had roamed the Southern Ocean as king and queen among beasts? Now they are just so much meat, blubber, and bone—a potential six hundred barrels of pure whale-oil to boost the factory ship's production.

Again we flag the cadaver for the towing vessel to re- cover, and continue with our search. Now we enter an area of much more solid ice. Heavy floes close in all around us, and it is time to get out into open water again—or so the whale-gunner seems to think. I watch him manœuvre his small but powerful vessel through great cracks in the ice, cracks which open up before us to make small, navi- gable channels lined by a complex construction of ice pinnacles fragmented to spear-like points. To the south- ward, the eastward, and the westward lies a vast wilderness of virgin white ice. The loneliness and awesome immensity of the scene depress our spirits. The whale-gunner curses loudly as an extra-large ice growler passes along the star- board side with a jarring noise.

"When in doubt always steer to the north-west," he says. "One always finds an outlet in that direction. But I don't think there will be any more blue whales to-day."

We nose our way back into open water, but icebergs seem to stretch to infinity. The whale-factory ship can be seen far to the northward. Smoke and steam, belching from funnels and exhaust pipes, mean that she is dealing with many dead whales.

The gunner turns to me with his Nordic smile. "Time for you to be getting back to your own job," he says. He reaches out a large, grimy hand and swings the engine- room telegraph to Full Speed.

3

The nations squabble over the spoils

LONG and patient efforts have been made over the past thirty years by many governments and their scientific advisers to agree upon and to enforce international regulations which would save the whale from extinction. The whole world is now covered by the rules and regulations of the International Whaling Commission which was founded in 1946.

Yet alongside these admirable efforts greedy over-exploitation of the whale population has continued. It is ironically and sadly true that to-day, despite all the regulations, the whale is in greater danger of extermination than ever. Over-fishing has set up a chain reaction. It has reduced the whales to such numbers that huge investment in whaling no longer brings in the former immense profits. This has created an entirely new balance of power among the whaling nations. And it threatens to undermine the work of the Whaling Commission.

Many shipowners of the former great whaling Powers have now realized that profits which were made soon after the last war are no longer there to be had, simply because the whales are becoming fewer and fewer. Some of these shipowners, having had the best of it for years, have sold out their vessels to the Japanese. A Japanese firm, in acquiring a British whale-factory ship recently, also bought with it for £2,150,000 a four-ninths' share of the British whaling quota. How much longer will Britain be represented in Antarctic whaling? She had only two expeditions in 1960–61.

Two nations have now risen to leading places in the whaling industry—Japan and the Soviet Union. Both of them have highly efficient whaling fleets with the latest scientific equipment, and both have economic systems which enable them to beat the former big Powers of the industry at their own game. Russia and Japan are self-sufficient to a degree which European nations never attained, for Norwegian seamen and whalemen formed a large proportion of the personnel of ships of other nations. The Japanese and Russians have all the resources they need, and the commercial profit-and-loss system which governs the whalers of Western Powers does not apply to them. They need the oil, and they are determined to get it.

The State-operated Russian fleets and the cut-price Japanese are now just waiting for the other Powers to get tired of the game. They can afford to wait. Neither is keen on international regulation of the industry. If the day comes when they have squeezed the rest of the world out of Antarctic whaling they will be able to make their own regulations or dispense with them altogether. Then it will be a race to the death to grab what remains of the world's priceless whale-oil, and the magnificent whale will soon be a memory of the past—as the elephant, the rhino, and the hippo are likely to be in Africa if ruthless exploitation is not checked. What is to stop it? I seriously question whether international regulations can do so.

The change in the industry is shown by these facts. In 1932, when the first attempt at an international agreement was reached between Britain and Norway, these two nations were the world's leaders in the whale industry. But in the 1960–61 season Japan had the highest national catch quota, Norway was close behind in second place, and Soviet Russia was third. Then, a long way behind, came Britain and the Netherlands.

It is generally agreed that the sperm whale was saved from extinction in the nineteenth century only by the development of electric light, which made sperm-oil for lamps obsolete. In this century it is almost certainly true to say that international regulations have saved some species of whale from total extinction. But for how long?

The history of the attempts to regulate the industry is long and tedious. It was not difficult to agree on principles for conservation, but it was extremely difficult to enforce them. It was fairly easy to fix a total catch limit, but not at all easy to get nations to agree on what share of the total each country's quota should be.

The first effort to save such a valuable source of food and profit as the whale was the signing in 1937 of the International Whaling Convention in London by nine governments. These nations agreed on opening and closing dates for Antarctic whaling, limitation of the size of whales to be killed, and the complete protection of lesser species. Despite this, four Japanese expeditions and one South African ignored the rules. In 1938 and 1939 the regulations were renewed and improved, but then came the War. For four years humans were too busy killing one another to have time to slaughter whales and a terrible toll was taken of the whaling factory ships and catchers which were turned over to war uses. The Norwegians began again with one factory ship in the Antarctic during the 1943–44 and the 1944–45 whaling seasons. And before the War ended plans were well ahead for resuming big-scale whaling under international regulations. The oil was desperately needed as food for a hungry and exhausted world, and shipowners knew that handsome profits awaited them. They built super factory ships to bring in the harvest. The whale population had enjoyed a brief respite from destruction, but it was not enough. Then was the time to halt all whaling for some years to enable the whale to recover from pre-war exploitation. But the commercial pressure was too great to resist. The next few years were a bonanza for the owners of pelagic whaling expeditions. Bigger and better ships were built, more and more catchers were employed, competition became fiercer and fiercer. More and more scientific devices were used, and wider and wider areas of the Southern Ocean were combed in the hunt. And for a time profits of nearly 100 per cent. on investments representing millions of pounds were made. The resources of the expeditions could be expanded indefinitely; but the whale population could not. It should have been clear to all that exploitation was running perilously near to extermination.

The fact was that the time for making fortunes in whaling by putting more and more science into the hunt was passing with each succeeding year. There weren't enough whales to kill at that rate. It was remembered by the old hands that the pre-war whaleships, usually old converted passenger or cargo liners which had seen better days, always returned home at the end of a season with a much better record for the number of whales killed and the amount of oil produced in a season than the post-war, specially built sea-factories which carried double the personnel and all the devices science could muster.

Credit must be given to the International Whaling Commission for an important step forward in conserving stocks when the nations decided at the end of the War to agree on a convenient unit for defining the number of whales caught. This was known as the Blue Whale Unit, or B.W.U., which laid down that one blue whale equals two fin whales, equals two and a half humpbacks, equals six sei whales. Previously attempts to limit catches by species had been difficult to apply. By fixing the largest rorqual, the blue whale, as the standard unit and relating the others to it, it became possible to apply an over-all limit to catches.

Before the War the nations had been killing about 24,000 B.W.U.'s a year; now the limit was fixed at 16,000. The aim of the regulations, which were embodied in the convention when the International Whaling Commission was set up in 1946, was exploitation without extermination. The threat of extermination was clearly understood by the Powers, as the preamble to the convention made plain when it stated: "The history of whaling has seen over-fishing of one area after another, and of one species of whale after another, to such a degree that it is essential to protect all species of whales from further over-fishing."

You may judge whether the international efforts were successful in the following fifteen years, from the remarks of Mr W. M. Fletcher-Vane, Joint Parliamentary Secretary to the Ministry of Agriculture, Fisheries, and Food, when he addressed the opening session of the 1961 meeting of the Whaling Commission in London. He said the conservation of the stock of commercially important whale species had become an increasingly pressing problem in spite of the Commission's efforts hitherto. This seems a clear admission that commercial greed had defeated all the good intentions of the international planners since the peril was recognized in 1946.

The total catch limit of 16,000 B.W.U.'s agreed to after

the War for Antarctic pelagic fishing was recognized as having no scientific basis in relation to conservation of stocks. It was guesswork based on what the operating companies thought the traffic would bear, and the results show that it was much too high a figure to safeguard the whale. In succeeding years it has been reduced to as low as 14,500, but in 1959 the catch limit agreement broke down over disagreements on national quotas. Norway and the Netherlands opted out of the convention, and the catch limit was suspended. The whaling countries agreed, however, not to exceed the size of the national catch limits they had fixed for themselves for the 1959–60 season, which totalled 17,780 B.W.U.'s. In fact, they did not reach this total in 1959–60 or 1960–61.

The figures of whales killed were:

1959–60: 15,512 B.W.U.'s; 1960–61: 16,427 B.W.U.'s

In this latter year twenty-one expeditions operated in the Antarctic—eight Norwegian, seven Japanese, three Soviet, two British, and one Dutch. But the figures given were not the total of whales killed in Antarctica, for they do not include sperm whales or the whales killed by the South Georgia land stations. To get the grand totals of Antarctic slaughter you must add 4173 sperm whales killed from factory ships in 1959–60 and 4681 in 1960–61; and from the land stations in 1959–60 768 B.W.U.'s and 89 sperm whales, and in 1960–61 830 B.W.U.'s and 134 sperm whales.

The International Whaling Commission does its best to supervise the industry, but it lacks full powers of compulsion. It acts only in an advisory capacity on behalf of the member nations, and meanwhile the nations squabble. Some are more interested in the wealth of to-day than in the treasures of to-morrow. Without a sense of obligation on man's part to the bounty of nature there can be no future for the whale. The treasure-chest is emptying.

The regulations are well-meaning, but they are a compromise between the desire for preservation and the greed for more gain. A serious attempt is being made, as I write, to provide the Commission at last with a complete scientific survey of whale statistics on which conservation could be based. Three eminent scientists, including one nominated by the Food and Agriculture Organization of the United Nations, are making a special investigation of whale populations to ascertain "how to obtain an increase in the sustainable yield of Antarctic whales." I hope they get the facts in time to prevent the last round-up.

Remember that nearly 50 per cent. of the female whales killed in the Antarctic waters each season are pregnant and that the reproduction rate is low. Only one calf is born in a little over two years of the female's life. Would any farmer kill off his stock in this wanton and ruthless way?

All seaborne whaling expeditions must carry inspectors. They are appointed by the government concerned and are generally axed naval officers. Their main duties consist in keeping a daily record of all whales killed by the catcher fleet. The length, sex, and species of each whale is noted; also, if female, whether she is pregnant, and the length and sex of the foetus. In addition, the position of the factory vessel has to be recorded, and the type of weather and ice conditions prevailing when the whales were caught. Regulations state that all whales killed must be processed within thirty-six hours and that all parts of the whale, except the intestines, must be processed. Nothing must be dumped into the sea. It is against the regulations to kill any blue whale under seventy feet in length or any fin whale under fifty-five feet. It is prohibited to kill any female whale that is feeding young.

The inspectors are on board to see that these regulations are carried out. That they have probably never seen a close-up view of a whale before their trip to Antarctica does not seem to matter. At the beginning of the voyage any species of whale, irrespective of sex, is just a whale to them. They have to learn as they go along. How much more sensible it would be if young biological chemists did this work.

Here at hand is what should be a biologist's dream—a 100-ton monster of blood, flesh, and bone, being dismembered every hour of the day and night. What opportunity for real biological research! Every facility is at hand for experimental work, and the vessel is fitted with large laboratory accommodation ideal for research and the gathering of scientific information. Yet the only person I ever saw interested in this work was an old doctor we had with us one season. Every forenoon, as regular as clockwork, he appeared on the working-deck armed with a large knife and attired in working-overalls and the essential spiked boots. He pottered around for hours, and nothing escaped his notice.

By the time the season ended there was little he didn't know about the anatomy of the whale. He was deeply interesting to listen to, and was the only boffin I ever knew who could speak from practical and scientific experiment. His only fault was that, in his thirst for knowledge, he made himself liable to be killed at any moment as he hopped around the whaling deck, dodging the various heaving wires and lethal hooks. Many a whaleman cursed him loudly as he shouted, "Look out for the wire!"

Our own scientific staff aboard the factory ship were far too busy with ship's work to worry about these matters. They had continually to test and grade the whale-oil as it came through the separating machinery. All whale products had to be tested for vitamin content and many other qualities. The boffins felt they had quite enough to do without messing about with whale carcasses on deck.

The chemists had a marvellous laboratory. I found them

one day, attired in their usual snow-white overalls, amid a forest of test-tubes and sample slides. A multitude of flasks of every size and description lined the bulkheads, and work-benches. Secured to permanent positions were such instruments as microscopes, tintometers, micro-scales, electric ovens, and all the paraphernalia of the modern biochemist. But I noticed that they were busy developing photographs.

Practical whalemen have little time for these intellectuals who dream up new ideas for scientific whaling.

4

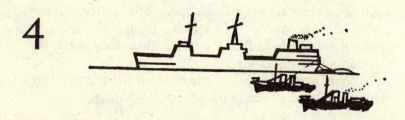

Fitting out for the Far South

Now I go back to the beginning and tell you how the great factory ships prepare for their fabulous voyages of profit to the Far South.

She looked an enormous and ungainly vessel as she lay alongside the Tyneside wharf, loading stores and equipment for yet another whaling season. She was one of two British whaleships built immediately after the War to replace to some extent the enormous losses suffered in the Battle of the Atlantic, and she had been successful right from her maiden voyage.

Imagine a very large ship, nearly six hundred feet overall, beamy and bluff-bowed, with navigation bridges practically overhanging the stem except for a huge cargo hold which was the main receptacle for whaling equipment and spare gear.

Immediately below the navigation bridges was the

accommodation for the Master, the deck officers, and the whale-gunners, with suitable saloons and smoke-rooms near by. From here the main, or whaling, deck ran clear of obstruction towards the stern for a distance of 360 feet. Although the area of this working-deck was about 30,000 square feet, it was not nearly big enough when whaling operations were in full swing.

Between the fore and aft sections of this vast deck was a built-up structure, aptly named by the crew 'Hell's Gate.' Here were housed the enormous steam hauling winches which hove the whale cadavers from the sea to the deck. Built into this superstructure were the trade workshops for carpenters, plumbers, boilermakers, blacksmiths, welders, and fitters. All these workshops were fitted with the finest of tools and repair machinery.

At the stern end two large funnels abreast of each other stood on the boat-deck over an imposing superstructure consisting of three decks. Here were housed most of the whaling personnel, in two- and four-berth cabins. Space, where there should have been space, was at a minimum around this boat-deck. Besides the conglomeration of life-boats and electric winch hoists, there was a large hanger which sheltered two helicopters.

A large hole, the whale-slipway, was cut away in the stern from the waterline to the whaling deck. The slipway sloped at an angle of about thirty degrees and was so huge that two locomotives could have passed each other on it with ease. Every whale we caught passed through this slipway as it was hauled from its ocean home to the deck of the ship for processing. Around the working-deck at strategic points were steam and electric winches, capstans, and steam bone-saws. Flush with the deck were manholes to the whale-boilers and '-digesters' which dealt with the whale-meat and -bone.

Below deck and stretching for three-quarters of the

entire length of the ship was the factory. This was an oil refinery afloat—a mystifying maze of machinery and electric motors. Pipe-lines of all sizes and in vivid contrasting colours seemed to run in every direction. Huge whale-disgesters and massive steam pressure boilers stood everywhere. At the forward end was a dehydrating meat-meal plant. This processed raw whale-meat into meal after the oil had been extracted. Another great plant was a liver-meal and oil extractor. Everywhere were pump-rooms, settling tanks, and electric conveyor belts. Two large rooms, each containing about a dozen centrifugal separators, were located one at each end of the factory.

Immediately below the factory deck were the cargo storage tanks—thirty-two of them, in sections four abreast. Each had a capacity of 620 tons—a total of nearly 20,000 tons. Engines and boiler spaces took up considerable room at the stern end of the vessel. Twin steam engines, developing a horsepower of 7300, gave a service speed of twelve knots.

The navigation of the vessel had every available modern aid. Twin radar sets could seek out danger in any weather. This was an enormous advantage in the ice-ridden waters of Antarctica. One often wondered how whaling ships managed to work in pre-radar days. We also had gyro compasses, radio-telephony, and world-span radio transmitters. A radio beacon sent out its automatic direction signal. The whale-catcher fleet could get their bearings from the parent ship at any time.

Altogether she was a well-found ship; soundly built and amply powered; well provided with navigational aids and safety devices. She was a ship to inspire confidence in all who sailed in her. Strong . . . safe . . . comfortable.

That, then, was our modern whale-factory, from which the smaller ships went out to hunt and kill.

I watched some of the crew sign on, men for every department of a pelagic whaling expedition. There were flensers, cutters, bone-saw men, seamen, and boys for the whaling decks. There were cookers, separator men, oil-men, and labourers for the factory. Many trades and crafts were represented. Many technicians were needed for electrical and radar equipment. Major repairs would have to be tackled if necessary.

The engine-room staff alone were far more numerous than on other ships. Besides the squad required for steam-ing and engine maintenance, a large number were needed to tend the huge evaporator plant which could produce 600 tons of fresh water daily from sea-water. Without this water a whaleship couldn't operate. Then there were the catering staff, butchers, bakers, cooks, and stewards.

Here and there I saw new faces . . . young, eager faces, full of expectation but showing little anxiety . . . bold, confident faces—these were the young lads about to set off on their first voyage to sea as mess-boys. That it should be a whaling voyage, and to the Antarctic of all places, did not seem to excite them unduly. Sixteen-year-olds have little imagination, and therefore know no fear. Soon, they fancied, they would be full-blown whalemen, earning all kinds of money. Hadn't they heard stories about the huge bonuses they were paid? So much for every barrel of whale-oil produced? A bonus even for every ton of by-products? They had great expectations and no idea of the savage, gruelling toil ahead.

The largest contingent of experienced British whalemen came from the Shetlands. Then there were groups from Aberdeen, Dundee, and Edinburgh. The Border towns and Tyneside were represented, and there was a small contin-gent from Wales.

Many and varied were the tales told by these whalemen when they got together after an off-season spell ashore.

Several of them, of course, were engaged in the fishing
industry when they were not whaling. They manned
trawlers and drifters. Others were tradesmen who returned
to shipyards and shore trades in the close season. The
majority did any casual work they could find until it was
time to go whale-hunting again.

As the summer waned and the leaves began to fall these
seasonal whalemen became fidgety and unsettled. The call
of the South was strong within them. They began to itch
for their adventurous life. They knew what it meant—
hard work under appalling and wretched conditions.
Despite the glamorous stories, it was an ill-rewarded job
in the loneliest place on earth. But here they were, all
ready and fit to serve. Just one more season, they told
themselves.

Our British bosun was an example. He had spent in-
numerable seasons in the South. He was well over six
feet, broad in proportion, and was of a type seldom met on
land. It seemed as if nothing interested him outside his
job. But behind the placid exterior there was a great amount
of common sense and vast experience. A strong personality
indeed, and he got the maximum effort out of his men by
using the minimum number of words. During the off-
season he always returned to his native Shetlands. He had
his land, and he had his fishing. His time was fully occupied.
He couldn't be bothered with whaleships—not in the close
season.

His usual greeting on arrival back for another voyage
was, "It's good to see you again, sir. This is going to be my
last voyage south. No more of this bluidy life for me! It's
back to the farm and the fishing." The same story, year
after year. I had long since come to the conclusion that as
long as there were whales in the Antarctic to hunt, to kill,
and to process, there we would find our cheerful and
ever-efficient bosun.

A skeleton crew of deck officers, engineers, and trades-men were employed throughout the close season They supervised the annual refit. Our vessel was a welcome visitor to the shipyard, and everybody did his best to get us ready for sea.

It was now all hands on deck as we loaded out stores and whaling equipment. This took four days, and twenty-four hours a day. Stevedores handled everything on board, and the ship's personnel stowed it.

A whaling expedition to Antarctica has to be victualled for seven months for more than 600 men, with no hopes of replenishment. Besides the parent ship, fourteen to sixteen other vessels are involved. All the stores for the whale-catcher vessels and other auxiliary ships have to be supplied from the big floating factory. So enormous quantities of meat and provisions are essential. Contrary to the com-mon belief, whaling vessels are well-found and compare favourably with the best-run ships of the mercantile fleet. Fresh vegetables soon become scarce, but this lack is made up for by pickled, canned, and deep-freeze varieties. Re-frigerator chambers are always loaded to capacity, but they are never big enough to last us. We carry great quan-tities of tinned meats, fish, and fruits.

To increase our fresh-meat supply we reverted to a custom of the old sailing-ship days by shipping fifty young pigs. A pen was built in the whale-slipway, and the porkers were looked after by one of the whalemen on the voyage. When we reached Antarctica, and before we began whaling, the pigs were killed and the home-fed carcasses stored.

Potatoes were a trouble because they took up so much valuable space. Carried in wooden crates (for ventilation) instead of the usual sacks, they were stowed nearly every-where—on deck, in the factory, and in the hold. They had to be turned over frequently and hand-picked to eliminate the rotten ones, and this took a lot of labour. As all store-

rooms were loaded chock-a-block, it was usually an
intricate job at first to get to certain essentials. As the
voyage wore on more space became available, and towards
the end of the season the storerooms were as barren as
Mother Hubbard's cupboard. Our Norwegian chief steward
had a large staff to control. Into his work went a great deal
of organization. A happy and contented crew were proof
that he always did his job well.

One season our provisions became dangerously low.
During the homeward voyage the situation was desperate.
It looked as if we should have to haul away and sail to
some South American port for replenishment. Fortunately
—or should I say, unfortunately for us—our refrigerated
chambers were fullen laden with whale-meat. This was to
be shipped home as an experimental food for silver foxes
being reared for their skins. The whalemen were the foxes
in the end! For the last seven days of the passage, until we
reached the refuelling port, we practically lived on whale-
meat. It was disguised in many ways—as sausage, meat
pies, or choice grilled steaks. To us it was still—whale!
One disgruntled whaleman tackled the chief steward.
"See here, steward," he complained bitterly, "if this whale-
meat racket carries on for much longer we'll all be breathing through the tops of our bloody heads." However, we
reached the refuelling port still breathing in the normal
way. The steward then made amends. We lived like fighting
cocks for the rest of the passage.

Deck, factory, and engine-room store requirements
were colossal. Take the deck department, for example. To
prepare whale-lines for the catcher vessels 240 coils of six-
inch Manilla and 260 coils of three-inch nylon ropes were
required. This, end to end, would have measured forty-
five miles. Huge quantities of flexible steel wire were also
stowed. Sizes ranged from six and a half inches down to
one and a half inches. During the outward voyage about

fifty men were continually employed splicing this wire
into strops and runners of many sizes and types.

Timber was another large item. About 60,000 square feet
were used in the season. The whaling deck had to be
completely sheathed over with two-and-a-half-inch soft
timber and, in certain places, with oak or other hard wood.
Frequent renewals to the sheathing were made during
whaling.

Then there were great stocks of harpoons, harpoon
grenades, gunpowder, firing screws, and time fuses. Spare
harpoon guns were carried, as well as spare propellers and
tail-end shafts for each of the expedition's catchers. The
usual paint, hardware, and stores of every description were
stocked for use of factory ship and catcher fleet. It was a
calamity if we could not supply anything that was required
by a whaleboat.

In the factory there were 120,000 hessian sacks for the
meat- and liver-meal we produced, as well as a great
number of five-gallon steel containers for liver-oil and
meat extracts. Steel plating, brass, copper, and iron ingots,
round steel bar, angle iron, and pipes of all sizes and
description were shipped for repair work. Large-scale
repairs often had to be done both on the factory ship and
in the catcher fleet. Our tradesmen, all of them masters of
their craft, usually had a busy time.

Imagine next the huge quantity of laboratory, medical,
and slop-chest stores we had to load. From the 'slops' the
650 men of the expedition could buy almost anything.
Take the cigarettes: about seven million were sold each
season, and seven million cigarettes are quite an item. Tip
to tip they would stretch nearly three hundred miles.
The slop-chest was run on a non-profit system. All goods
were of the best quality and were cheap.

At last every item was safely aboard. The day came when
we were ready to leave for another whaling season in the

South. As we cast off many of us waved to families or friends on the quayside. Other whalemen looked down on these poor landlubbers and felt a lofty and soul-satisfying superiority. Tugs pulled us gradually into midstream, and we were off down-river to the open sea.

5

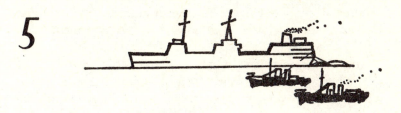

Our Norwegian friends

OUR first passage was across the North Sea to Tönsberg, in Norway, where we were to pick up our Norwegian personnel. Here we were always greeted with much excitement. As soon as the anchor was down the whalemen came clamouring on board, all eager to sign on and begin work. Our stay at this port was never more than twenty-four hours.

These men were of similar type to our British crew. All had spent many seasons in the Antarctic, both with sea-borne expeditions and at land-based stations. All seemed pleased to be on board again, ready to face another tough season after five months' enforced stay ashore. The same faces year after year: the flensers, lemmers, cutters—the real specialists of deck work—and the cookers, separator men, and more tradesmen for the floating factory. They were not so fortunate as our British whalemen: there was

little or no temporary work for them in the small towns
of Norway during the close season. These men had to
make a whole year's money in the seven months they
were away. Many of them were to man the speedy whale-
catcher ships. They were mates, engineers, and seamen,
well trained and highly skilled at the job of hunting and
killing the whale.

And then came the whale-gunners—the aristocrats of
the whaling ports. These men commanded their own
whale-catcher vessels—strong, successful men who had
received their training from their fathers before them, for
their trade is a closed shop.

Tönsberg, Sandefjord, and Larvik are the main whaling
ports of Norway. About one-third of the population of
these towns gets a living from whaling or trade connected
with it. When ships sail for the South every year they leave
silent towns behind them; towns deprived of a big part of
their male population. It is easy to imagine the joy which
greets the return of the whaling fleets. In the small old-
world town of Tönsberg you can't get away from whaling.
There is a statute of the renowned whaleman Svend Foyn
in one of the main squares. The harbour and fjord were
littered with whaleboats at this time. You could imagine
yourself 7000 miles away in the far reaches of Antarctica.

The town even smelt of whale, for no home in Tönsberg
is without its whale-soap. From the well-kept and scru-
pulously clean houses the smell of whale pervaded the
street. No respectable Norwegian whaleman would come
home from a voyage without his barrel of home-made
whale-soap. Here and there, in the well-tended gardens of
houses belonging to once-famous whale-gunners, giant
arches made from the jawbone of some baleen whale
towered some fifteen feet over the gateways. In the hotel
lounges and bar-rooms the conversation was only of
whale, of whaleships, and of the men who manned them.

Even on market days, when families from the surrounding countryside paraded the small town, the whale-gunners were pointed out as if they were film stars.

Again more stores and equipment to load on board. Much of the gear used by the whaling nations of the world is covered by patent rights which are the property of Norway. The harpoon gun is an example. It was invented by Svend Foyn, whose fame still lingers in all the whaling ports of Norway. This gun, together with the whale-slipway, completely revolutionized whaling. They made possible the mechanized and streamlined industry we have to-day.

While Britain and the United States persisted in hunting the humpback and sperm whales by the older methods, the Norwegians quickly saw the possibilities of the Svend Foyn gun and the explosive harpoon grenade. They went after the much larger and less buoyant whales that were known to inhabit the waters of the Southern Oceans—and they quickly gained supremacy. In the First World War Britain and America stopped all whaling. Not so the Norwegians. They built up both their whaling fleet and their knowledge. They introduced the whale-grab—an ingenious device that could get the 100-ton cadavers on to the deck in a matter of minutes, thus obviating all outboard flensing. By the end of the War Norway was far ahead of the other whaling nations. To-day she is losing that lead to Russia and Japan, though she still helps to man the expeditions of other nations.

And what of these other whaling nations of to-day, these countries whose whaleships steam South every year to hunt the mighty mammals? What does it bring them in kind? I listened one day with a sort of Olympian detachment to our medical officer explaining to one of the boffins the various uses of whale-oil. His facts seemed to be a little mixed. Whale-oil is used as a food. It is used largely in the manufacture of margarine and all types of fat. Inferior qualities are used in the manufacture of soaps. Whale-meat, equal in quality and taste to a prime beef-steak, is being canned and marketed by both Germany and Japan. By-products include cattle and chicken feeds, bone meal, face-creams, leather dressings, fertilizers, and manure. Sperm-oil, not to be confused with the ordinary whale-oil, is non-edible, and is used in the manufacture of candles and finer lubricants. Both oils have great glycerine contents.

Approximately two hundred and seventy thousand tons of whale-oil is processed each season by the whaling fleets of the combined nations. This huge total is collected in a period of ten to twelve weeks, depending on how long the seasonal quota holds out. From one unit each factory ship will produce approximately one hundred and five barrels —seventeen tons of whale-oil. Without going into statistics, it can be mentioned that, during the last ten years alone, processed whale-oil to the value of £250,000,000 has been taken from the icy seas.

I have often wondered why Australia and New Zealand have never had a finger in this rich pie. It is not because they are uninterested in what happens in Antarctica. Each claims vast segments of the frozen continent. They have one or two shore-based stations around their own coast-lines, but they seem indifferent to the treasures that are being taken from near-neighbouring waters. Now it is much too late for them to catch up.

But back to Tönsberg. Our decks, as well as our holds and factory spaces, were now covered with stores of every description. Huge stacks of timber towered over hundreds of drums of lubricating oils and crates of potatoes. Coils of wire and Manilla rope, required during the voyage south, were stacked over a wide area and covered with tarpaulins. Elsewhere were machine parts, cases of machinery and electrical stores, spare whaleboat propellers, and tail-end shafts. The Norwegians had built up mountains of new harpoons on the deck, as well as scores of barrels of salted meat and pork. Our forward hold was now loaded to capacity with whaling gear. Some of the steam pressure boilers, used in the cooking of whale, were even brought into use for storage. Out of this organized chaos would come complete efficiency.

We were fully equipped for the South, stored and manned for another whaling season. That it would be a successful one was the fervent wish of every whaleman on board. Much would depend on the weather and the ice conditions. No two seasons were alike.

And now it was good-bye. As we slowly steamed down Tönsberg Fjord, martial music blaring from our loud-hailers, hundreds of small boats, nearly gunwale-deep with relatives and friends of our Norwegians, sailed with us towards the open sea. Strange as it may seem, Norwegian women seem to like to see their menfolk sail off to sea—especially their whalemen.

Slowly but surely we left the little boats far behind in our wake. There was now only one stop between us and South Georgia. At Aruba, off Venezuela, we would have to load our usual supply of 20,000 tons of bunker fuel. So we set our course to the Far South.

6

Antarctica—here we come!

FOR a landlubber it would be an education to see how whalemen go about their daily work. Here there is no 'go-slow,' no lead-swinging. A tough job lies ahead, and each man knows the score: he is there to see it through. Each is a cog in a large wheel and essential to our expedition. We carry no reserves. Whalemen need no prodding—only direction and advice. No sooner had we cleared the land than gangs were at work everywhere.

Let's go on a tour of inspection right through the ship to see what our crowd of six hundred were doing—how they earned their money. On the whaling deck seamen had begun the job of splicing whale-lines for all the catcher vessels. Each line consisted of six coils of six-inch Manilla rope and one coil of three-and-a-half-inch nylon foreline, a total of 790 fathoms, or three-quarters of a mile long. Two complete lines were required for each vessel, one fitted to either bow. They would be renewed, or partly renewed, during the season. The nylon foreline was frequently renewed. Some whaleboats used as many as sixteen during the brief season.

A large squad of flensers and cutters, working in pairs, were splicing hundreds of the wire runners and tail strops which we should need on deck and in the whaleboats. These men were masters of the art of wire-splicing, an art gradually becoming obsolete among present-day seafarers. Working with great dexterity, speed, and skill, each pair could get through dozens of splices during a working day. When you are whaling the least sign of fraying in a wire, or of a jagged edge, means that the strop must be instantly condemned. The whaleman works in blood and guts. Pricking fingers or hands with a jagged wire always leads to blood-poisoning—or at least to painful swelling. So great care was necessary to see that all working-gear was in new condition.

Under the guidance of the ship's carpenters a gang had begun laying the new wooden deck which would completely cover the whaling deck. This work was done with uncanny precision: every plank had to fit into its proper and exact position. Electric saws were in constant use, cutting the timbers into the required size and pattern. All whale-boiler openings, which were flush with the main deck, were fitted with portable hatch-planks made from oak or similar heavy wood. When this work was completed the whole expanse of deck area was as smooth as a billiard table. This was essential for the constant use of flensing- and cutting-knives when we began dismembering whales.

Elsewhere on deck working-parties were busy on whale-boat essentials. Others were overhauling or renewing deck and factory equipment. Fitters were employed in the factory spaces. All machinery was opened up, examined, and overhauled if necessary. Considerable work was involved with the meat- and liver-meal plants. The meat-meal plant in particular was a huge and complicated mass of machinery and required constant maintenance. Whale-meat, in pieces of about a foot square, was fed continuously through electrical hoggers and pulped to a soggy mass. It was then conveyed by a system of worm-gears through various processes, which included treatment tanks where steam and boiling water were introduced. From here it was conveyed through expelling machinery, which pressed the oil and glue waters out. On it went—into revolving steam driers. After the drying operation the meat was milled into a very fine meal. This was immediately bagged and stored in the cargo tanks. I can well remember when this plant went into operation for the first time. Our factory vessel was brand new—just delivered from the builders. In order to school the ship's personnel in the use of this plant, a mathematical chemist (the definition was his own) and an engineer were sent from the makers to go south with the expedition. Great results were expected, and we on board were a little worried how best to cope with the bag a minute expected from each spout. But things didn't work out this way in actual practice. On its first and sub-sequent trials the plant was like a Hell's Cauldron—a maelstrom of whirling machinery, with steam hissing and worm-wheels clanging and grinding, at a tempo diabolic in its sound. Knives, which were supposed to cut the meat in cubes, didn't function at all. Looks of disdain, contempt, and self-complacency appeared on the faces of the personnel at this huge contraption of ambiguity. The mathematical chemist was told, in no uncertain terms, where he should put his contrivance .... Still, the teething troubles were eventually overcome, and to-day the plant turns out its seasonal production of approximately 3000 tons in a matter of ten or twelve weeks.

The electricians were busy men as they went about

testing and overhauling the electrical motors. There were 300 in the factory spaces alone. Generators and switchboards would have done credit to any moderate-sized town.

On the tank-deck below the factory work was going on with equal efficiency. It was the domain of the tank bosun —another Shetlander. There were only eight men in his gang, and their job was in the cargo tanks throughout the season. It was an unnatural job, an unhealthy one. They saw daylight only at meal-times. Most of the time they worked under huge arc lights. All were volunteers, for this had proved the best way to organize a gang for such work.

It was the tank gang's job to see that the cargo tanks were clean and fit for the carriage of whale-oil. It meant a vast amount of cleaning. The tanks were steamed and washed under pressure, then scraped and dried. Pipe-lines had to be tested and the proper suctions introduced. The job had been simplified in recent years by the introduction of mechanical washers and cleaning solutions. Before a tank was passed as ready for whale-oil it had to be inspected by the chief officer, the chief engineer, and the senior chemist. Contamination of the whale-oil by even a slight amount of fuel oil would have been a catastrophe. Each tank of 600 tons would contain oil worth about £50,000, and we might fill it in a twenty-four-hour period of whale-processing.

Far down in the bowels of the ship there was the ship's laundry. Why the designers put a steam laundry down there was hard to understand. No words can describe the heat and humidity of this torture chamber. For ten shillings per voyage (the money went back into the crew's welfare fund) all whalemen were entitled to free dobying done by experienced laundrymen with ultra-modern equipment. What did it matter if one was nearly always minus a few items on the return of the bagwash, or if one received back a pair of John L. Sullivans belonging to the portly chief cook instead of one's own light-weight trunks. It all came out in the wash, and was ironed out by a suave and diplomatic laundryman.

Now let's go up into the open air again. High in the forepart of the ship were the navigation bridges. Here, as in the engine-room, watches were being kept by the junior officers with a regularity and vigilance known only to seafarers.

In the trade workshops activity was just as strenuous on the voyage south as it was on the actual whaling grounds.

Blacksmiths' shops have always held a strange fascination for most people. The brawny men at work here beside forge and anvil were always hard at it throughout the voyage. Besides the equipment required by factory vessel and catcher fleet during whale-hunting, there was a miscellany of gear to be maintained.

On the whaling grounds anything up to one hundred and thirty harpoons could be used during one day's operations. These were extracted from the whale carcasses as they were dismembered. It was the blacksmith's job to straighten and rethread the grenade heads—quite a task, when one considers that each harpoon weighed nearly one hundred and fifty pounds and they were sometimes so buckled after use that the rear end was at right angles to the headpiece.

The ship's slop-chest, or shop, was open twice weekly. No shopkeeper could have wished for better customers. Cigarettes were sold by the thousand; chocolate bars by the gross. It was not until the end of the season, when we signed our slop accounts, that we wished we had been non-smokers or a little less sweet-toothed. Some people will buy anything! The same people lined up at the store week after week. It wasn't as if they needed anything. They just had to buy something—a tie, maybe, or a couple of shirts, or a pair of shoes they would never wear till they got back home. It made them feel good and more civilized. One day they would use the treasures they had bought aboard.

Close to the navigation bridges was a workshop where the radio mechanic worked on his own. He was rarely seen outside his shop and little known to the majority of the crew. But he laboured throughout the voyage to maintain the complex equipment for all vessels of the fleet up to the severe strain imposed on them. Radio transmitters, radio-telephony, direction-finding apparatus, and radar all came under his care. It wasn't a spectacular job, or physically a strenuous one, but it was vital to the success and safety of the whole expedition.

When we were on the whaling grounds any radio defect or failure aboard the catcher vessels was instantly reported to the parent ship. The old mechanic was alerted, and as soon as the whaleboat came alongside he went aboard with his little black bag of testing instruments and tools. He made a quick examination and a few tests. If the trouble could not be put right at once there was no more delay. A valuable catcher could not be held up. So a complete replacement unit was called for. It was always ready. The old apparatus was quickly disconnected, the new one wired up. The ship was ready to go back to work. The discarded unit could be repaired at leisure and made ready for another emergency.

Another hard-working fellow aboard was the pig-man. His charges always thrived on the southward voyage, and by the time they were killed, just before we reached South Georgia, they were huge. They were a welcome addition to our fresh-meat supply.

One season we arrived at South Georgia with twelve pigs still alive on board. It was decided to add twelve more from the shore station. The idea was that they should be kept alive until the Christmas and New Year festivities. The shore pigs were to be loaded during the early hours of the morning, and I had instructed the pig-man that he was on no account to mix them with the factory ship's pigs. A pen, made of empty oil drums, was to serve as a temporary sty. It had been a pleasant night-shift for the pig-man. While waiting for his new charges he had a few drinks with several of his South Georgia friends. This led to an exchange of anecdotes, and he settled down to make a night of it. The working-gang got the pigs on board just after midnight without much fuss or bother, and the leading hand went looking for the missing pig-man.

"Where do you want the pigs?" he inquired, when he found him. The pig-man stopped in the middle of an amusing story, put down his glass, and glanced round at his island friends. "What the hell!" he exclaimed. "Can't I have a couple of hours' leisure without some trouble? Put the bastards along with the others. Where the hell would you put them?"

So the shore pigs were mixed with the others. Immediately there was pandemonium and chaos. The stillness of the night was shattered. There were blood-curdling screams as the pigs began a battle royal. Blood began to flow. The pig-man, now quickly on the scene, added to the uproar by getting into the sty and striking out in all directions with a capstan-bar. Officers, whalemen—even the manager—rushed from their disturbed sleep to see what was happening. Who had been killed?

The now thoroughly dispirited pig-man, seeing the manager of the expedition eyeing him coldly, tried his best to explain. "It's all right, Kapitän, it's all right! Give them five minutes more and they be very good friends. They won't make any trouble! Not any more!"

Resuming our tour of the ship, we come to the galley

spaces—the domain of the cooks, the butchers, the bakers, the store men, the mess-men, and the mess-boys. This was a vast culinary establishment where work went on around the clock. Breakfast at 8 A.M. had to be repeated at 8 P.M. Dinner at noon was repeated at midnight. So the cycle moved. Like the rest of the crew, the cooks and the butchers were of two nationalities. One day the diet was thoroughly British; the next it was Norwegian style. It all went down the same way, and, except for the few who suffered from 'whaling stomachs,' every one seemed to be happy.

The galleys were well equipped with labour-saving equipment. From the huge oil-burning ranges to an all-electric bakery, everything was of modern design and streamlined for efficiency—except for the electrical fish-fryer. This apparatus was the pride of our Norwegian chief cook, and its chromium-plated exterior always gleamed brightly. It had only one fault. It wasn't allowed to function. Its use was prohibited. When it was first tried out everything electrical on the navigation bridge went haywire. The steering gear functioned erratically. The gyro compasses tried their best to seek another polarity. The radar screens showed terribly distorted pictures. It took over an hour for a crowd of harassed deck officers, engineers, and electricians to locate the trouble. The fish-fryer was connected up to the navigation circuit!

It was not all work on the voyage south. Even whalemen have their hours of leisure and recreation, especially on passage to and from the whaling grounds. As we entered warmer latitudes, with temperatures beginning to soar, they soon put up their canvas swimming-pool. Every second evening a movie performance was given on deck. This was attended by most of the crew except the watchkeepers who were on duty. On the whaling grounds the film show was twice weekly. By the end of the voyage each of us had probably seen every programme about a dozen times—and there were twelve different programmes, all the latest issue. Musicals seemed the most popular long films, but we equally enjoyed the 'shorts' and cartoons.

Every encouragement and facility was given to welfare aboard ship. A small committee was formed at the beginning of the voyage. It was their duty to find ways and means of relieving the monotony of the passage. Young whalemen, too, had great opportunity to further their education and knowledge. Navigation classes were held daily from 1 P.M. to 3 P.M. on the voyage to and from the South. Classes were open to both Britons and Norwegian and were presided over by junior officers of both nationalities. Many young lads went on from here and eventually gained certificates.

The ship's library was always well-stocked and was used by everybody. There were several thousand books in both languages. Some had been presented by the shipowners, others were bought out of the crew's welfare fund, and many were on loan from the Seafarers' Education Services. Our librarian-cum-film-projectionist was the deck store-keeper. He was a Jack-of-all-trades and a magician who could produce from his store anything from a sewing-needle to a kedge-anchor. But he was also an excellent seaman, an all-round whaleman of the younger school, as willing as he was capable.

Housey-housey, or Bingo, was a favourite pastime. It was played on deck in the evenings under huge flood-lights. Entry fees were paid with cigarettes, and the games were usually attended by scores of men at every sitting.

Once during each passage out and back we had a sports meeting. Great was the rivalry between the two nationalities—an Olympic Games in miniature—and the excitement aroused was terrific. The executives of the ship always hoped that the final scores would turn out fairly even, to avert bad feeling. There were excellent athletes among the crew. With proper training facilities some would have been first-class. Main events were: 100 yards flat; 80 yards hurdles; high jump; long jump; and tug of war. The 100 yards sprint and the high jump were the most keenly contested, but the tug of war usually caused great excitement—and hilarity. Gambling, by means of cigarettes, went on throughout the proceedings. The book-makers, of course, always came off best.

No people is more fiercely patriotic than the Scots. One year the sports were advertised on the public notice-board as "Norway v. England." Somebody had dropped a big brick. The notice was promptly torn down and the follow-in substituted:

A Scotsman is never an Englishman.
But a Scotsman is always British.
The announcement should therefore read: "Great Britain v. Norway."

A five-a-side football tournament was once organized, but the first game was the last. One player received a broken leg; another had severe head injuries.

The greatest highlight of the voyage south was undoubtedly the stage show. It was the climax to our steaming in tropical waters and always took place south of the equator: after this event we soon ran into the colder latitudes. All the principals gave many hours of their spare time in rehearsals. We had a full and competent accordion band. The show was directed and produced, year by year, by the same two men, a factory whaleman and the chief chemist. Both had experience of theatricals. A large stage was built and fitted with coloured lights and decorated with national flags. Loudspeakers and micro-phones were installed.

The show was always a huge success. Enjoyment was shared by the actors and 'actresses' and by the large and

noisy audience. I have seen far less glamour on the pro-
fessional stage than we had here in our chorus of twelve
young whalemen billed as "The South Latitude Girls."
Their version of the Can-Can brought the entire house
down. We also had a lugubrious comedian whose visage
barely altered as he put across his songs and patter. His
stories might well have been banned by any board of
censors, but they always got by the ones we had on board.
Where did the costumes come from? Your guess would be
as good as mine.

Our up-to-date whaleship had come a long, long way
from the days of the Aberdeen, Dundee, and New Bedford
whalers; from the days of the great Melville and his *Moby
Dick.*

7

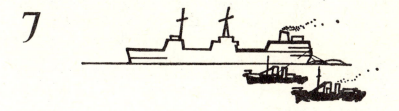

Of whales and boffins

THE boffins had found their sea-legs and were now making personal preparation for the start of the whaling season. 'Boffins' was the name we gave to the non-practical whalemen—the intellectuals of the whaling industry. The chemists, the whaling inspectors, the doctor, and any other specialists aboard were lumped together as 'boffins.' The senior chemist, or production officer, was usually the spokesman for this group of collar-and-tie whalers.

They knew—or thought they knew—everything. Arguments among themselves were loud and long throughout the voyage. Besides whaling and everything connected with whaling, they treated us to verbal treatises on such subjects as nuclear fission, parliamentary procedure, world affairs, and birth-control. Meal-times in the officers' saloon were the time and place for the opening gambits. We practical whalemen soon left the table. We had more immediate and important affairs requiring attention. Within a few minutes the boffins were roaring across the table at one another like a crowd of seaborne bulls.

One day the talk was about the Soviet Union. Tempers, not easy at the best of times, seemed to get a little frayed between the doctor and one of the whaling inspectors.

"I—I tell you. I should know! Hell! I've been there!" the doc kept shouting and repeating.

All of a sudden the tumult was silenced by a voice roaring into the open door of the saloon. "Why the hell did you ever come back? If you'd stayed there people around here might have got some bloody sleep!" It was one of the deck officers whose watch was below.

The doctor had an easy time in the early stage of the voyage. Surgery hours were from 9 A.M. to 10 A.M. and from 6 P.M. to 7 P.M. daily. But during whaling operations he was on call at all hours of the day and night. Accidents were frequent, and his work was sometimes heavy. He had the help of a male nurse. Doctors served only one season. It was unusual for them to repeat the voyage. Many were out for new experience—and money! That they got experience in the waters of Antarctica I can well vouch for. I wouldn't be so sure about the money.

The hospital and surgery were well fitted out. Some doctors would rather do anything than pull teeth. Others seemed pleased to do so. I have often watched them at it, and I always advised them not to be too good at dentistry. A husky seaman went to see the doc one day about a large molar that was causing him pain. I happened to be in the surgery at the time, so I sat back with some amusement.

"Does it pain very much?" inquired the medical officer, as he probed around the decayed tooth.

"Aye, doctor, it's gieing me hell," answered the Shetlander.

The doc kept on with his probing, taking no notice of

the yells of the patient. Then he went to his work-bench, filled a hypodermic, and returned to the dental chair. A few hasty jabs around the tooth drew a loud howl from the patient. Armed now with a large pair of forceps, the doctor waved them in front of the whaleman, grabbing him strongly at the same time.

"How does it feel now?" the doc shouted.

The patient looked up with a woebegone expression and replied, "The pain's gone now, sir."

"What, gone?" shouted the doc, as he wheeled around the dental chair.

"Aye . . . aye, the pain's gone now, sir."

The medico pondered for a few moments. "Hell!" he exclaimed. "What's the use of pulling the bloody thing if the pain's gone? You come back to-morrow if it still aches."

The whaleman got away as fast as he could, and that was the last that was seen of him around the surgery. I suppose the whole crew quickly heard about "that bloody quack."

The psychology was good. The doc had few dental patients during the season. But if at the beginning of the voyage he had extracted teeth painlessly he would have gone down as "a damned good dentist," and would have been bothered throughout the voyage. In fact, towards the end of the season many whalemen apply to have all their teeth extracted so that they can have dental plates fitted at once on arrival home. After all, we do live in a welfare State. Even the foreigner takes advantage of that.

The boffins always seemed to wangle a trip whale-hunting with one or other of the expedition's catcher vessels. Some whale-shooters would in no circumstances allow trippers on board their vessels during the whaling season. But the doctor, the whaling inspectors—even lesser mortals—would often make their own personal contacts and would enjoy a couple of days away from the factory ship, providing the weather was good.

Usually got up in an outfit that would have been a credit
to the film version of *Scott of the Antarctic*, they would go on
board the respective whaleboats with enough gear and
paraphernalia for a three months' voyage instead of the
usual two days. By the time the trip had ended and the
whale-shooter had killed several whales the boffins were
lecturing on whale-hunting with an authority rivalling
that of Captain Ahab, and speaking more dogmatically
than any whale-gunner with a mere twenty years' experience behind him would dare.

Somehow, every season, the boffins were always glad to
return to the factory ship. Invariably they overstayed their
welcome on the catchers.

Not all of them carried extensive equipment. I remember
one who faced the rigours of an Antarctic whaling season
with a grip and about as much gear as would see him over
a week-end jaunt to Blackpool. I found him one day waiting to be lowered to the catcher vessel that was alongside
refuelling. "Hell!" I exclaimed. "You're not going away on
a whaleboat for a couple of days like that?"

He looked at me rather pitifully and answered, "Well—
I—I haven't got a hard-weather coat. Can—can I borrow
one?"

I took pity on the poor fellow. "Sure, you can borrow
one," I told him. "Get one out of my room. There are
two in the wardrobe. You can take either of them."

He soon returned to the bunkering platform with my
best coat and was lowered to the deck of the whaleboat
below. He was much more suitably dressed now and might
compare favourably with Alan Ladd in the film *Hell below
Zero*. He looked like a real live whaleman.

For the rest of the season my efficient, workmanlike
hard-weather coat was used on all occasions. It went from
catcher to catcher as the boffin carried out his series of
experiments. The season ended, and the coat saw service

in South Georgia as the boffin accompanied various fishing parties and similar expeditions. The coat and the boffin were inseparable.

We left for home. Just before we arrived in the United Kingdom the boffin came to my room. "Thanks for the use of the coat," he said. "It's been a great help to me. I will have it cleaned at home before I return it to you." I thanked him, and he eventually left the ship. I still await the arrival of the coat. I told you whalemen were a crowd of mugs! Still, perhaps that boffin will one day read this book . . . .

8

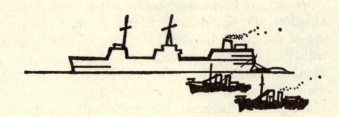

South latitude

THE outward voyage was running its course; we had rounded the north-east corner of Brazil, crossed the equator, and were now on a direct course for South Georgia.

It had been the usual busy thirty hours in Aruba. In this short time we had docked, loaded 20,000 tons of fuel-oil, and got under way again. Fuel-oil at this port is loaded at the rate of 1500 tons an hour, so the loading gang had little or no relaxation. It was a battle from start to finish to work the loading valves. We were no super-tanker, with all valves nicely arranged on deck, painted in vivid scarlets, greens, yellows, and whites, and looking rather like ornamental pieces. In our factory ship the cargo tanks and loading valves were two decks below the main deck, with all valves placed in the most impossible positions. When it was time to stand by to change into a different set of tanks somebody had to crawl on all fours beneath some electrical motor, steam pressure boiler, or such encumbrance. Loud were the curses (in two languages) as heads were cracked or legs bruised in the process.

Our whalemen had a riotous time on their one evening ashore. It was a last fling before settling down to the grim business ahead. Anglo-Norsk relations were, however, always of great cordiality, and crews were never troublesome.

Two hundred and eighty miles a day is a steady and handsome speed. We rapidly shifted our parallels of latitude—especially on this southerly course. Soon we were out of the tropics, across the thirties, and into the 'roaring forties.' The temperature had taken a sudden downward plunge, and skies were mostly overcast. Our whalemen began to put on heavier clothing. Many began to grow beards. During actual whaling at least 60 per cent. of the crew sported beards. I never could quite fathom the motive. Vanity? Or laziness? Or a desire to keep the face warm?

Lifeboat and fire drills were religiously carried out during the voyage out and back. When we were whaling we had little time to worry about such trifles. Saturday, 4 P.M., was the usual time for musters and drills. All hands, except the watchkeepers, had to turn out and go through the exercises. Some of our crew didn't like these drills, and many tried to dodge them. This was never repeated after the first couple of Saturdays because all hands were kept waiting at stations until the offenders did arrive.

One amusing story came out of such an incident. It was just after the beginning of the last World War. This was the only time I ever saw a perfect lifeboat muster. The whaling season had finished, and, to get every one accustomed to his lifeboat station, we called a muster outside the usual schedule. As we were steaming in fairly safe waters many of our crew arrived at stations in a lacka-daisical manner, growling to themselves at having to turn out on their first free afternoon for some months. Many were missing entirely.

Next morning, Sunday, at the request of the whaling manager, we called another boat muster. There was no advance warning; only three people were in the secret—the manager, the chief engineer, and myself. We ordered that the gun should be fired and the engines stopped, to make the drill more realistic. At six o'clock in the morning the four-inch breech-loading gun went off with a thunderous roar. Alarm bells rang throughout the ship. The engines came to an abrupt stop.

Action! . . . I could never have wished for a better turn-out. It would have done credit to any man-of-war's crew turning out for battle stations. Hundreds of whalemen, many of them nearly naked, others in various stages of disarray, stampeded and jostled one another as they frantically tried to fasten their life-jackets and line up at their proper stations.

"What's happened? What's happening?" I heard one whaleman anxiously inquire of another. I watched him trying to contrive an expression of ease and languor sufficiently exaggerated to calm his leaping nerves as he glanced anxiously round in the forbidding morning light.

"Och, it's just anither of these bluidy boat musters," the Shetland seaman replied.

The whaleman looked at the Shetlander with an expression about as happy as that of an aged St Bernard dog, and, as he violently shook his head, I heard him mutter angrily to himself, "Boat muster! Another of these boat musters! What a bastard of a ship!"

We often got talking about Antarctica; of the exploration and scientific parties that now seek to probe some of the secrets of this vast white continent, and of its future

uses to mankind. We even got into arguments with the
boffins about it, especially during periods of relaxation
when we all gathered in the smoke-rooms. Of course, the
boffins knew it all.

There is no doubt about it, activity is now intense round
the coastline of this last unexplored continent. Great
Britain, U.S.A., Russia, France, Australia, and New Zealand
have all established near-permanent bases, and this step is
only the prelude to greater assaults in the future. Explorers
and scientists have opened up more of this continent in
the last two years than all the previous expeditions combined. American, British, and Russian aircraft have flown
across great areas never before seen by man. Enormous
mountain ranges have been charted. During the International Geophysical Year land stations were set up and
maintained far south into Antarctica, equipped with fabulous modern scientific equipment. Concentrated research
and explorations were carried out, and it is now definitely
possible to establish land bases. It is said the aims are purely
scientific, but they must inevitably have political significance. The situation bristles with difficulties.

Antarctica is an area of about five million square miles.
Some geographers believe, rightly or wrongly, that it
consists of many large islands and seas that have been
overwhelmed by a glacial sheet well over three thousand
feet thick. Present-day charts present it as a roughly circular land mass, with the South Pole as its centre. Incised
into this frozen land are two major seas—the Weddell and
the Ross. They lie on opposite sides of the continent, and
they narrow the breadth of the continent at their nearest
points to one thousand six hundred miles. Both of these
seas are navigable at certain times, but not without great
difficulty and hazard.

Nowadays the risks are too great for seaborne expeditions
to penetrate the ice-packs of these seas in search of whales.

Too much time is involved in getting through the dense ice. Chances of failure and financial loss cannot be taken in these competitive times. I talked to an old Norwegian flenser about whaling in the Ross Sea, because I knew he had served with two expeditions in these waters.

"Yes, those were the days, all right," he said eagerly. "The first whaleship that ever penetrated the ice-pack and got back into the Ross Sea was the *Sir James Clark Ross*. She battered her way through nearly solid ice for days on end, with her brood of catcher vessels trailing and labouring behind her. We were lucky if we ever saw any water. Nothing but ice, a great wilderness of white ice.

"The whale-shooters of those days weren't afraid of ice —not like nowadays. The farther they can get away from the bloody stuff the better now, or so it seems. It's front-page news when some ship manages to get into the Ross or Weddell Seas. The more flamboyant the expedition, the greater the publicity. Their ships are built for the job too. It's a lot of fuss about nothing."

The old-timer was referring to the *Sir James Clark Ross* expedition of 1923–24. The parent ship was an old cargo liner, converted to whaling, but without the modern whale-slipway, She went in search of whales—and dividends—but got neither. This was not the fault of the expedition's leader, Carl Anton Larsen. His vision and foresight paved the way for this era of modern seaborne whaling. He seems also to have prepared the way for the utter and complete extinction of the whale.

Larsen had pioneered the whaling industry in South Georgia and took an active part in whaling in the South Shetlands. It was on the advice of Captain R. Amundsen, discoverer of the South Pole, who believed that whaling in the Ross Sea would be profitable, that the *Sir James Clark Ross* expedition was fitted out. Larsen got the required financial backing, and his ships left Norway. They steered

towards the ice-pack by way of Tasmania and Macquarie
Islands. They had great difficulty in pushing through the
heavy ice that blocked the way to the comparatively freer
waters of the Ross Sea. Steering due south to the Bay of
Whales, the area recommended by Amundsen, they didn't
see a single whale. Then the weather, which had been
extremely good, gave way to violent and continuous gales.
There was no shelter, no harbour. The few indentations
along the coastline were packed with solid ice. Next came
fog; then more gales. By bitter irony, whales were now
plentiful, but the weather made it impossible to handle
them alongside the ship. The flensing teams did their best,
but it was hopeless. Larsen realized that some method would
have to be found to get the whole whale carcass aboard
the factory ship. So the idea of the present-day slipway was
born.

But trouble dogged Larsen in the Ross Sea. The waters
became rich with the brown plankton that is the baleen
whale's diet, but the expedition was doomed to failure
because of the weather and the ice. Large sections of the
ice barrier frequently broke away, to become islands
drifting in the prevailing current. Often and without
warning, the whole of the ice face shattered on a front
miles wide and 'calved' in enormous masses, pushing its
way from the polar plateau. The barrier stretched for
thousands of miles east and west, but only at certain points
could it be approached by open water.

Larsen decided to go home. Winter was setting in. Even
the open seas began to freeze. The whales had gone, the
seals were scarce; even the birds had begun their migrations.
The morale of his crew rapidly deteriorated; they had
suffered enough. The expedition forced its way north
again. Anton Larsen was beaten, but he was certain that,
with new methods, a seaborne whaling expedition could
still be successful. Experts scoffed at his ideas, but he was

proved right. Such were the iron men who opened up the whaling industry of Antarctica. The *Sir James Clark Ross* expedition produced only 17,000 barrels of whale-oil from two hundred or more whales—a pathetic return for so much hardship, danger, and financial investment.

We were now preparing for our arrival in South Georgia. All deck and factory work had been completed. Working-lists and shifts were posted up, and the whalemen put the finishing touches to their equipment. Flensers, cutters, bone-saw men, and lemmers had their knives sharpened to a razor's edge by a cutler employed solely for this job. Working on a twelve-hour shift, he would grind knives throughout the season. Each knife was mounted on a four-foot wooden shaft. It looked rather like a hockey-stick.

The slop-chest was doing a roaring business. It was essential to wear knee-length leather boots when working on the whaling deck. These boots were studded with heavy steel spikes to enable men to move about the treacherous decks when they were slimy with blood and blubber. All whale-catcher stores and equipment were arranged on deck in separate lots so that each boat crew could pick up its quota quickly when we arrived in South Georgia. The storerooms at this time looked as though they had been blasted by a bomb. But the storemen knew just what they were doing. They could find anything from a diving-suit to a plain pair of tank boots. Yes, most whale-factory ships carry diving equipment, but the tradesman who acts as diver has usually little experience of diving. He signs on as such at a nominal extra monthly salary, and the ship's executives earnestly hope that no underwater repair work will be needed on the voyage. Once in South Georgia I was approached by a complete stranger who informed me he was the new diver and fitter. He inquired about the diving equipment, its whereabouts, and its condition. I called the deck storekeeper and instructed him, "You'd better take some men and look out the diving equipment. The new diver is going to test the gear. Work under his direction." The storekeeper nodded and hurried off. I forgot about the order I had so hastily issued until about an hour later, when I saw a large group of whalemen peering intently over the side. With great hilarity and many shouts of profane advice, they were watching some one working below. I remembered about the diver.

I looked down to the deck of the catcher vessel moored alongside. The storekeeper and his gang were pumping air and tending the lines of the diver. His feet, encased in the regulation diving-boots, were high in the air out of the water. His steel-helmeted head was pointed straight downward to the sea. His right hand was moving in a circular motion which presumably meant, "Keep pumping."

"What the hell is happening?" I shouted.

"I don't know," the storekeeper answered nervously, as he glanced aloft. He pointed towards the diver's feet and gave a sort of defeated shrug.

I gave a quick nod to the Shetland bosun who was standing near. He went immediately into action. Seizing the end of a nylon foreline that was lying handy, he made a running bowline and threw the end down to the deck of the whaleboat. "Put this round his bloody legs," he shouted. This was quickly done. The crowd of whalemen, led by the bosun, quickly hauled the diver up feet first and deposited him on the deck of the catcher vessel.

The crew thought it all a huge joke. It didn't seem so funny to me at the time. The diving-suit was pumped so full of air it looked like a barrage balloon. Never again did I have any faith in the so-called whale-factory ship's diver.

In the last days of our passage south whale-gunners showed impatience and traces of 'whale-sickness.' Time hung heavily with them as they tramped the decks for many hours of the day and night. Now and again a distant feathery spout of a whale would be seen. This always caused excitement. "How is it heading?" was the invariable question. The young whalemen dashed from their work to look. They didn't realize they would see a couple of thousand whales right there on deck before the season ended. The youngsters swaggered about, feeling important, excited, and impatient. The elder whalemen were just as bad. No work was done until they had decided to their own satisfaction what type of whale we had sighted and the direction in which it was heading.

Whalemen can be as naïve about whales as landlubbers. I remember, not very long ago, a show touring Britain with a lot of publicity. The exhibit was a whale that had been washed up on a beach. An enterprising showman had obtained possession of this cadaver and, by means of injecting formaldehyde into it, had succeeded in keeping it in fairly good condition. It was carried on a special trailer truck and shown off as the "original Moby Dick." Admission charges were made, and the advance publicity was so good that the show drew large crowds as it passed through many towns for a one-day stand. I have a happy recollection of watching many of our most experienced whalemen waiting their turn in the queue to see this rotten cadaver. Some of them had, to my own knowledge, worked on probably thirty thousand whales during the long years of a whaling life. And those were whales at least five times larger than the one on exhibition which they were prepared to pay a shilling to see.

Talk about 'a busman's holiday,' or that other proverb, 'fools and their money . . . .' I should know—I was in the queue.

We passed the first icebergs in latitude 46° South. From now on we should see them constantly. We had already sighted our first albatross, and often had a dozen or more gliding over the ship. These giant Southern Hemisphere birds have an amazing wing-span—up to twelve feet. They follow a ship for hours, sometimes for days, and then suddenly they are gone. One moment they are planing their way right alongside us, then, without the flicker of a wing-tip, they are far astern in our wake. Their absolute immobility in the air amazes every one who sees them for the first time.

Skua gulls, Wilson's petrels, and Cape pigeons also greeted us, sometimes in groups of one hundred or more. When we got down to whaling we should have them with us in thousands. The Wilson's petrel is a funny little fellow. He can barely fly. His wings flutter constantly, and he never comes to rest. We feel sorry for him, for he seems out of his element alongside the other ocean birds. The skua gull can be dangerous. Once I was out deer-stalking in South Georgia and had climbed several ridges away from the foreshore, when I was attacked by a couple of skuas. They zoomed at me in repeated vertical dives, and it was only by good luck that I kept them at arm's length. I used my rifle as a club, but they just flattened out as it was swung at them. I got away as quickly as I could, and later found that I had been near their nest.

Early one morning as we turned out we saw a familiar landmark towering high ahead of us. It was South Georgia. This island was described by Sir Ernest Shackleton as "The Gateway to the Antarctic." It was a huge mass of snow-capped mountains. For four hours more we steamed steadily towards it. It seemed to rise higher and higher into the sky.

Here we were to renew old acquaintances as we met our over-wintering crew who had been left behind from the previous season. We should have five days to requisition our catcher fleet. Then southward again towards Antarctica.

9

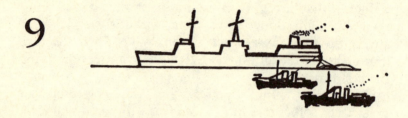

Gateway to the Antarctic

THE island of South Georgia lies about 1000 miles to the eastward of Cape Horn. The coastline presents a rugged and scowling appearance. Jagged, razor-edged rocks jut out of the sea off a deep and savage foreshore. In the interior glaciers run down huge valleys as tremendous pressures are exerted by the new layers of ice which continually form. The waters abound with life. During the last half-century untold wealth has been reaped from both sea and foreshore.

Seals and sea-elephants litter the shore and rocks in vast numbers. In certain months of the year multitudes of penguins appear out of the icy waters of Antarctica and converge on the coast of this island to rear their young. Fish swarm in the bays and inlets during the summer. Reindeer roam some of the coastal hills, and sea-birds find sanctuary in the nooks and crannies of the rocks. The only vegetation on land is a type of tussock-grass which grows scantily in limited areas.

Masses of kelp grow up from the sea-bottom and reach the surface, to spread out and cover the rocks with gigantic umbrella-like leaves of dark brown. Throughout the Southern Ocean this kelp is continually on the move. Each storm tears away large masses from the sea-bed, and currents carry it away on a voyage round the world.

South Georgia is a dependency of the Falkland Islands group—a British Crown Colony. There is a resident magistrate in charge. His staff consists of only one customs-official and one police-officer. They, with the staff of the Government radio station and their families, are the island's only permanent residents. The seasonal whalemen, nearly one thousand two hundred of them, are employed by the three whaling firms that operate from land-based stations. They are British, Norwegian, and Argentine interests. Each season their whale-catcher fleets take from the neighbouring waters approximately four thousand whales. These yield about thirty thousand tons of whale-oil and by-products worth nearly £3,000,000. The Argentine station is allowed, under licence, to kill an annual quota of seals, but this industry is becoming a thing of the past.

The exploitation of South Georgia by large business interests has seen an era of much slaughter and indiscriminate killing of both seals and whales. First came the sealers, British and American schooners manned by men of many nations. These ships anchored in the small bays and inlets, and their crews were soon ashore, setting up the cauldrons for boiling out seal-blubber. Gangs went out on the foreshore to club the basking seals. A few quick strokes of the knife and carcasses were stripped of their blubber and left to rot. Then on to the next bay or inlet for further slaughter. This wanton butchery soon reduced the seals, and the industry had its day. Every accessible island in the Southern Ocean was exploited in the same way.

With the invention of the harpoon gun, man was now able to hunt the much larger whales. The era of open-boat whaling and the hand harpoon, described so vividly by Herman Melville, was closed—never again to return. Big business took over. Land-based stations were hastily built, and operations began from South Georgia. Profits were instantaneous, and the ever-grasping hands reached out southward—to the South Shetlands.

The next phase was the development of the floating whale-factory. Seaborne whaling had arrived. But it was not until several years later that the first whale-slipway came into use. Until then all flensing and cutting up of whales had to be done alongside the parent ship. This was a most hazardous operation, and the factory vessel had to stay always in sheltered waters. So they used the vast areas of open water that lay within the ice packs of the Southern Ocean. Ships penetrated far into the ice for shelter.

At certain periods Deception Island was used as a base for whaling operations. Factory vessels entered this natural harbour and moored stern-on to the shore with both anchors down and leading ahead. The catcher fleets scoured the adjacent waters, and their kills were towed back to Deception for processing. Fresh water was plentiful, and work went on regardless of weather conditions. Deception Island is 1200 miles to the south-west of South Georgia, but is accessible only at certain periods of the year.

Such is the history of the industry on which our ship was now engaged. The bay we entered shelters three harbours where land-based whaling is carried on. The bay itself is very much like a Norwegian fjord, not only in its mountainous aspect, but in its large and wide expanse of dead water. Our base was in a small, narrow cleft, an ideal location. There could be a howling gale out at sea, and we should know nothing about it in this shelter. Only from one direction was the station vulnerable. If the wind blew from this point it came directly off a large glacier, bringing icy blasts and squalls which roared through the gullies and reached a howling crescendo as they passed over.

A shore-based whaling station is a sordid habitation. Scores of squalid and dilapidated wooden huts and buildings clustered as near as possible to the foreshore. A curious ozone smell pervaded the whole area—a smell which only a whaling station can produce. Here and there tall iron chimneys belched out smoke or steam. A large wooden ramp sloped from the water's edge, to form a vast working-area where whales were flensed and worked up. Round this area on three sides were sorry-looking buildings of wood or metal sheeting, housing whale-boilers and -digesters. Steam hoists hove the whale-blubber and -meat to the roofs of these buildings, where it was deposited in the open maws of the boilers. Large oil-storage tanks seemed to stick up everywhere.

Off the whale-ramp a couple of mooring-buoys enabled the station whaleboats to leave their dead whales there ready for processing. Thousands of birds squatted in the water all round, feeding off the scraps and bits of organic matter that floated around. They gorged so much that they couldn't fly.

Our own whale-catcher fleet were moored line abreast facing the foreshore, awaiting our arrival. They were squat, formidable-looking craft, as imposing as warships with their freshly painted hulls and superstructures. During the close season each vessel was given an extensive overhaul by teams of engineers, mates, and seamen who were left behind for this work. They had every facility at hand for the job, including the use of a floating dry-dock.

There were more than three hundred men employed at this base during the close season. They were the over-winterers who had volunteered from the season before. Most over-winterers were overjoyed when the factory vessel arrived back in South Georgia. They received loads of mail, old friends were welcomed, and, best of all, they went back to the excitement of another whaling season. Then—homeward-bound.

As we moored off the broken-down wharf (everything is dilapidated about a whaling station) our whaleboats came buzzing alongside us like a swarm of angry bees, all jockeying for position to load stores and equipment quickly. But our mooring could take us up to three hours. Six-inch wires and fourteen-inch coir hawsers had to be hove on board and made fast to the mooring-bollards. Our anchor cables were hove ashore and shackled to embedded ground anchors. Elsewhere nylon ropes and mooring-wires were fastened to shore- and mooring-buoys.

The magistrate and staff were immediately on board; *pratique* was granted, and the job of signing off the catcher personnel from the factory ship was begun. Later they signed on their own vessels. Work was interrupted frequently by the greetings and gossip of old friends. News from home was eagerly sought by these over-winterers, who looked a tough and disreputable gang of characters after their winter's sojourn in South Georgia. Whale-gunners and crews soon took over their catcher vessels, and the work of requisitioning them was started immediately. We handled four boats at once.

First the whale-lines were hove on board and coiled with scrupulous care in the line lockers. Their ends were rove through a complicated system of blocks, directly leading to the bow leads on the gun platform. This system of blocks culminated in heavy buffer or accumulator springs fastened to the keel of the ship. The springs took the sudden shocks and tension when a whale was harpooned and fighting for its life. All aboard went the harpoons, harpoon points, gunpowder, time fuses, firing screws, flags, flag-spears, air-spears, whale-buoys, knives, and a thousand other essential items.

The whale-harpoon with its pointed grenade attachment is just over five feet long and, as I have mentioned, weighs 150 pounds. The nylon foreline is spliced into the rear end of the harpoon. As soon as the weight comes on the line as the whale dives, a steel barb attachment opens out at right angles and prevents the harpoon from being dislodged. The whale-gunner now has the animal on the full scope of his line. He then uses his own technique to 'play' and 'land' the animal. A killer harpoon is often used for the second or third shot. This missile is much lighter. It is fitted with the same explosive head, but has no barbs and requires no whale-line.

As each vessel was equipped she was topped up with fresh water and oil fuel. Provisions were loaded, and everything had to be done to enable her to start hunting as soon as we left South Georgia. Technicians and tradesmen were kept busy on each ship. Radar, radio-telephony, radio transmitters, direction-finding apparatus, and whale-detectors all had to be tested and serviced if necessary. The whale-gunners who commanded these hunting ships kept a squad of tradesmen working right up to the last minute. They always found fault with something and had to have alterations. But at last each was completed, and the gunner took her into the bay for trials. Compasses and other equipment were tested. The harpoon gun received special attention and was experimented with for hours at a stretch. The gunner fired at a floating target while putting his ship through the most intricate of manoeuvres.

The parent ship then had to make final preparation for whaling. All derricks and other standing gear had to be

positioned and made ready. The whaling deck was now
completely bare except for the gear required for the working-up of whales. It looked like a miniature football-field.
Down in the factory spaces machinery was tuned to the
highest pitch of efficiency. We had discharged several
thousand tons of fuel to the shore station. This gave us
space to take on board additional fresh water. Water was
precious. Without it the factory would come to a standstill. And we still had to evaporate five hundred tons a
day to keep going on full cooking capacity.

South Georgia water is probably the finest in the world
—no spa excepted. It comes directly from the glacier and
is, of course, icy-cold. It has a pungent taste and is milky-
white, especially if there is great humidity in the atmosphere. The whalemen call it South Georgia gin, but it has
no kick in it.

We spent our evenings with our over-wintering friends.
Home topics were always the most interesting to these
men who had been away for over twelve months—a year
of heavy toil in one of the farthest corners of the earth.
But conversation always returned to whales, and to the
prospects that lay before us. With a bottle or two of
'Monkey's Blood' laced with sufficient South Georgia gin
the evening was full of warm comradeship.

The annual football match between the seagoing whalemen and the shore-based men always took place at this
time. No Rangers *v.* Celtic Cup Final could raise more
excitement. Odds were usually with the shore-based
whalemen. They had much more practice. The game was
always enjoyed, not only by a boisterous crowd, but even
by the numerous Adélie penguins which always turned up
when something was going on.

One memorable game was between the British and
Norwegian land-based whaling stations. Excitement was
intense throughout the first half, and as the teams turned

round at half-time with the British eleven leading by the only goal the supporters of both sides yelled encouragement. Above the din we heard a fierce argument between the rival whaling managers.

"I'll bet you we equalize," roared the manager of the Norwegian station, as his team, pressing all the time, narrowly missed a scoring chance.

"Like hell you will," answered the Norwegian who managed the British station. "Like to bet?"

"Sure I'd like to bet. I'll bet a blue whale we get the equalizer."

"Right." The bet was accepted without hesitation.

A rough second half ended without any addition to the score.

"Now you owe me a ruddy blue whale," the official of the British whaling station prodded gently.

"And you'll get it," was the answer.

Next morning a Norwegian whale-catcher vessel arrived at the British station, towing a large blue whale. The bet was paid in full. Quite a bet, too—perhaps one of the biggest ever made on the chance of a goal being scored. More than two hundred barrels of whale-oil could be processed from this one cadaver, with a market value of about £3000. Never mind. What the hell, the property wasn't theirs . . . .

If permission could be obtained from the resident magistrate a reindeer-hunt was organized during the factory vessel's stay in port. Reindeer were first introduced to South Georgia many years ago by one of the Norwegian firms. They multiplied a thousandfold. To-day the herds roam the coastal hills, feeding off the scanty tussock-grass, their only source of food.

The boffins always managed somehow to wangle a place in the select hunting party. Officially there were about twenty of us armed with service rifles, the property of the ship. But I have seen many others who had managed to

beg, borrow, or share a rifle and gatecrash the show. I
once noticed a Shetlander with a rifle that would have
dropped a wild elephant at 100 yards' range. The station's
service boat, an old catcher vessel, was requisitioned to
take the party to the most likely scene. They were landed
on the foreshore by lifeboat.

Against the brown-tinted rocks of the mountain-sides
the reindeer were hard to pick out. Like all gregarious
animals, they always seemed to be on the move. They
travelled slowly, a short ambling gait, usually in an ex-
tended file that followed some predictable pattern. They
halted at frequent intervals to graze.

The general strategy was for the hunter to move in
line abreast at right angles to the foreshore. When a group
of reindeer were sighted the object was to encircle them
on three sides, leaving the seaward position clear. An effort
was then made to beat them into a position as close as
possible to the foreshore before going for the kill. If the
plan worked a huge bag could be assured, and there would
be no trouble in getting the carcasses back on the whaleboat as the lifeboat could be manœuvred close to the
position. But if reindeer were shot at random on the hills
the whole party became disorganized, and it was often
impossible to get the kill back on board.

One reindeer-hunt in which I took an active part returned
with a poor day's bag. We had been landed on a likely
foreshore, but had tramped for miles without encounter-
ing the least sign of life. The disappointed hunters wandered
off singly or in pairs in every direction. Suddenly about two
dozen of the animals broke loose from a sheltering crag.
A shout went up, and some one fired. Within a second the
whole company followed suit. The cross-fire was terrific.
One hunter had his rifle shot right out of his hands. Every
one seemed to be in a No Man's Land, being plastered with
lethal ammunition.

If time permitted in South Georgia we sent a vessel out on a fishing trip. The outing was always successful. It showed a handsome profit by providing our chief steward with at least a dozen meals for over 600 men. Although fish swarm in the bays and inlets during the summer months, the larger ones are farther out. Sea-birds gave us a good indication of where the shoals were. As soon as the whaleboat got over such a patch, down went the lines. Within seconds the fish were being hauled on board in vast numbers. Ripper hooks seemed to be the best proposition. No bait was required. Within a few hours several thousand large-sized cod-like fish were caught.

The skipper of the service boat, who often led such expeditions, was a character. He was rather small and tubby, and he always went about with a cherubic grin. He could well have been a character from one of W. W. Jacobs' novels. Although born in Norway, he was British by adoption and had spent most of his life in the island of South Georgia. He often reminisced about the 'good old days."

His boat was an old and battered whaleboat, but to the old skipper she was the last word in luxury and efficiency. No private yacht could have had more care lavished on her. For his ship he would beg, borrow, or steal if necessary. He had to be a Jack-of-all-trades to carry out the jobs that came his way. One day it would be towing, the next perhaps a demolition job. It was all the same to him. He went about his work with the same smile and was always efficient.

I once went with him, as a passenger, to the Government post at Grytviken. Dense fog set in soon after we left the whaling station, and it turned into a real pea-souper.

"Do you think you can make it?" I inquired rather anxiously, as I stood alongside him on the small navigation bridge.

"Sure, sure I can make it," he answered sharply, as he swung the helm hard over to starboard to avoid a large, pinnacle-like rock that had suddenly loomed up ahead out of the gloom.

"Hell!" I exclaimed. "Take it easy, skipper. Take it easy. We can't see very far."

He grinned. "Oh, it's all right now. Twelve minutes more and we will be at the entrance to Grytviken. He was pointing in front and taking his time from a clock. I looked at his chronometer. It was a rusty and battered alarm-clock.

But, sure enough, after twelve anxious minutes he again swung the helm over to starboard, steadied, and reduced speed. Out of the gloom appeared the entrance to Gryt-viken Harbour. It was excellent navigation, but I dread to think what could have happened if the alarm-clock had stopped or the engineer had reduced the engine revolutions.

We cast off the remaining hawsers as the twin engines were manœuvred slowly astern, and our hulking whale-factory ship, laden to capacity, emerged from the narrow cleft of a harbour which had been our home for five days.

The moment of departure had arrived—the moment for which five months of intensive and highly organized preparation had been made. We were, in all respects, ready to begin an Antarctic whaling season.

Our whale-catcher fleet lay drifting around the bay, waiting for our departure—fourteen modern, high-powered vessels, efficient as any naval task force. Their loaded harpoon guns gleamed in the early-morning sun. Whale-boats Numbers One and Two had preceded us by twenty-four hours. Their job was to scout out the whaling prospects. We swung in the bay. With a farewell series of wails on the siren we headed for frozen waters.

10

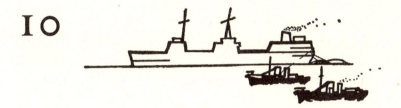

Frozen waters

AS we left the island of South Georgia behind us and turned our bows towards the south-east, our whale-catcher fleet fanned out ahead of us over a wide arc of the horizon. Although the baleen whaling season did not begin for two more weeks, it was permissible to hunt the sperm whale at any time. Now we entered that part of the world which still lies in the grip of the Glacial Age; a vast region with the most savage climate man has ever endured and defied. There is nothing to be seen here but the fiercest of seas and ever-changing ice.

From December to mid-February there is no darkness. At night, long after the sun sinks below the western horizon, the sky remains suffused with light. Ice conditions varied from hour to hour as we slowly steamed ahead. Here and there we met huge Antarctic barrier icebergs—gigantic, flat-topped floating islands that were once part of the ice shelf that rings the Southern Continent. I have seen one in the Weddell Sea up to forty miles long and towering out of the icy seas to a height of nearly two hundred feet. Its area was probably about a thousand square miles. And remember that only one-fifth of its volume appeared above water.

Scattered ice-packs and thousands of smaller icebergs lay directly in our path as we wallowed behind our catcher fleet. Everywhere there was absolute silence. It seemed to be the cumulative silence of millions of years. To the voyager who sees these waters for the first time the sensation is that of being on another planet. The erosive action of winds and seas has carved the ice masses into weird and fantastic shapes. With the help of a little imagination you see cathedrals and palaces, or old-time windjammers under full sail hurtling towards you. But, unlike the mirages of the desert, these visions are not imaginary. They are made of ice as hard as granite.

An Antarctic seascape has been described as "a grave-yard of gigantic marble-white tombstones." But it is their unearthly colour which gives them such amazing life and beauty. At a distance they look white, but as you approach you see they are a blend of whites, blues, and greens. In the doomed roofs of monster caverns hewn by fierce seas into the hearts of the icebergs glowing pinnacles rise as if they are part of a giant tapestry. Sometimes the bergs are pierced through, and catcher vessels have sailed through them to the other side.

The hull of the factory vessel threw weird shadows over the surface of the virgin ice-packs as we slowly pushed our way through the channels. There was a loneliness here that gripped the heart; a peacefulness too, and a menace. It frightened, yet fascinated. Above all, it emphasized the utter insignificance of man.

A really close-up view of an Antarctic iceberg is a never-

to-be-forgotten sight. By infinitely slow dissolution year
after year it has broken away from some terrifying glacier
of the Southern Continent, probably bringing, embedded
in its mass, a great deal of earthy matter. It is this deposit
of rock or earth which gives icebergs a great variation of
specific gravities. The average is about 0·8. The loss of
gravity is due to the amount of air enclosed in the volume.

Icebergs diminish in size in three ways—by calving, by
melting, and by erosion. An iceberg is said to have calved
when it cracks and a section breaks away. Melting always
takes place at the waterline. Erosion is caused by wind and
sea. As the iceberg calves, fantastic shapes float away. They
are of translucent blue, green, and white. The weird blue
dominates. Few people have seen this tremendous sight. I
once had a close-up view of it. The first indication that the
gigantic mass was about to calve was a series of ear-shatter-
ing noises. Great cracks began to appear on the face of the
berg. Then there was a dull and thunderous explosion as
the berg was rent asunder into four main sections. Smaller
segments crashed into the sea, disappeared for a few
moments, then rose again like pinnacles. Ice in the form
of growlers littered the sea for a wide area. We watched
this spectacle in silent awe.

Orders were now transmitted to the catcher fleet to
begin the hunt for sperm whales. At once the whaleboats
broke into lively and businesslike communication with
one another. They reported regularly to the factory ship,
where, on the navigation bridge, their bearings and distances would be plotted and all activities noted. No naval
task force could have been a more complicated organization to handle. All important operational signals were
transmitted in code so that we gave no news to other
expeditions. We had now set watches in two shifts—each
of twelve hours. From now until the season was over

work would go on throughout the twenty-four-hour day.

Although blue and fin whales are found throughout the Southern Ocean at all times, it is only in scattered areas that the sperm whale is seen. We waited for the first whales with gear and apparatus tuned to perfection. The few sperm whales we killed before the opening of the whaling season proper always provided good training for the crews of factory vessel and whaleboats. They enabled the executives to check up, under working-conditions, the efficiency of the plant. Last minute adjustments could be made if necessary before the rush began.

Sperm whales in the Southern Ocean are bulls only. They have an average oil yield of about 100 barrels—seventeen tons. Whalemen don't like working with sperm. The job is tough and the oil yield moderate for the work involved. These whales are blue-black, and the blubber is tough and resisting. The head is nearly half the length of the entire carcass, with a rectangular shape and rounded contour. This monstrous head, so awkward to work, is full of spermaceti, a wax-like substance which immediately solidifies when it is broken out. If you take a large handful of this jelly-like matter and press it like a sponge, a thick flow of pure spermaceti will ooze from your fingers, leaving nothing behind except a few rough sinews.

Separating the skull from the head-case is an intricate and sometimes dangerous job. It is always done by the first flenser. Armed with a knife with a twelve-foot shaft, he hacks at the tough, resisting tissues as two winches heave the head-case and skull in opposite directions. As they separate spermaceti blows out in all directions. The men working near scurry to safety. The hilarity is great if some unfortunate gets caught in the descending slimy spray which solidifies as it meets the cold air. The men are callous about the discomfiture of others, but just as callous about their own. A curse—and on with the job.

When the blubber and head are removed the carcass of the sperm whale is insignificant. The meat looks dark and soggy. There is not much bone to contend with. The stomach contents are sometimes interesting. Sperm whales, unlike the baleen, can swallow quite large objects, and their food consists mainly of cuttle-fish. To obtain this diet the sperm has to dive to great depths. There are other large, ungainly, translucent fish in the stomach, of no known category, dredged up from the sea-bed. The whale's body often has battle-scars which suggest tremendous fights in the deep between hunter and prey.

At rare intervals ambergris is found—mostly in small quantities. Only once have I seen a really large find—a lump weighing over one hundred pounds. Ambergris is formed by a diseased condition of the whale; it always has fragments of cuttle-fish beaks embedded in it. The theory is that the irritation of this hard substance sets up a sort of cancerous growth in the whale's gut. Ambergris is some-times found floating on the sea, or washed up on a fore-shore after being ejected from the whale. It was once a very valuable commodity because of its ability to intensify the power of perfumes. To-day the same result can be got by synthetic means, so ambergris has lost nearly all its commercial value. Small quantities can still be marketed. It is a hard, waxy substance of a dull brown and has little odour of its own.

A story, once quoted by a famous perfumery firm, tells of a remarkable find of ambergris when its value was still high. A young woman was walking on a beach on the coast of Peru, when she decided to sit down and rest on a small boulder close to the water's edge. When she resumed her walk she found her dress was badly stained from the boulder. She sent the dress to a firm of cleaners, and some days later an executive of the firm visited her to inquire if she could remember where and how the dress had become stained. She took the man to the beach where she had walked and soon found the boulder. As the executive had guessed—it was ambergris.

There are still a lot of unanswered questions concerning the sperm whale. For example, why has no female ever been killed in Antarctic waters, though two thousand or three thousand bulls are killed there every season? And why haven't bulls been killed along the coasts of Chile and Peru where females are seen at all times? They must mate somewhere. Nobody yet knows where.

From the Galapagos Islands, running south along the coasts of Peru and Chile, female sperm whales were abundant not so long ago. To-day, like the Antarctic baleen whale they are rapidly decreasing in numbers. Pre-war expeditions took a heavy toll from this area of roughly two million square miles. It was an entirely different type of whaling from ours to-day. Factory vessels, with their brood of catchers out ahead of them line abreast and roughly five miles apart, steamed at full speed until whales were sighted. The sperm whales were usually in pods of a hundred or more. The factory ship stopped engines and lay drifting while the whaleboats went in for the kill. Within a few hours the whole pod was slaughtered, and the surrounding waters were covered with floating cadavers. They put up very little fight for life. The female sperm is much smaller than the bull—rarely more than forty-five feet long.

The work of processing these beasts was quite different, too, from that in Antarctic waters. It was simply slaughter and greed. A team of men were continuously employed at the whale-slipway, heaving the whales on board— sometimes as many as four at a time. The whale-grab was never used. On the foredeck scores of whalemen, stripped to the waist in the intense heat of the Peruvian coast, would deal with the cadavers. It was just a case of stripping them of their blubber, removing the head with its store of sper-maceti, and then dumping the remainder of the carcass back into the sea. And they now wonder why the number of sperm whales has declined in this vast area.

Beaches and foreshores of Chile and Peru must have been littered with mangled carcasses from this wanton slaughter. The birds and the sharks did well. Hundreds of sharks hung about round the factory vessel all the time. Some were seen, with mouth agape, catching the blood that was running from the scuppers. This cannot happen now. Laws have been tightened, and all whales must be completely processed. The Governments of Peru and Chile keep watch for any infringement of these inter-national rules. And they have several of their own, as witness the seizure of a modern whale-factory ship some years ago with her whole fleet of whaleboats. The action was fully justified.

I I

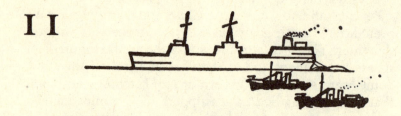

The temperamental gunners

WE always found ice conditions most severe around the vicinity of the South Sandwich Islands. Huge packs of heavy blue ice lay fast between the islands. Soon they would break up after the winter's freeze, drift away with the prevailing wind and current, and finally erode or melt. We used to try to pass to the southward of this group and proceed along the ice edge in a south-westerly direction.

The South Sandwich Islands form a curious chain. They run in a north-and-south direction from Traverse Island in the north to Thule in the south. And what a miscellany of names they have—Traverse, Zavodovsky, Lascov, Viskoi, Candlemass, Montagu, Bristol, Thule. They looked more like icebergs than islands, with their snow-clad peaks rising into the clouds. The depth of the surrounding waters averages two thousand fathoms, so they rise from the ocean-floor to a height of fourteen thousand feet. They are of volcanic origin, and Candlemass Island is still active. Like the island of South Georgia, they are dependencies of the Falkland Islands. Their only inhabitants are the various species of penguins, seals, and birds that make their homes in these waters.

Weather and whaling conditions were usually good in this area at this time of year, and whales plentiful—but we never knew how long this would last. They could be in abundance one day and gone the next.

Most evenings we had several of our whale-catcher fleet alongside for refuelling. Using a whale as a fender, they would moor alongside, and operations began at once. Whaling equipment was always loaded, and the vessel was usually under way again within half an hour.

Now and again, when weather was bad and there were no whales available as fenders, fuelling operations had to be carried out from the stern. The factory ship steamed slowly head to wind with the fuelling hose trailing astern. The catcher vessel came up from the stern, picked up the hose, and the refuelling was done with both vessels under way.

A few days on a catcher ship was a great adventure, even to men with vast and varied sea experience, and outranked any other thrill connected with modern whaling. Life may seem hard and tough on board the factory ship, but it is much more so on the catcher vessels. There it is a continuous fight—men against the sea, men against the elements, men against the ice, men against the largest animals known to mankind. There is no let-up. For ten to twelve weeks all catcher personnel are under great physical strain. Sleep is taken only in cat-naps during the first half of the season. There is no darkness, and whaling goes on all the time. During the latter half of the season the weather is mostly too severe for rest.

Different whale-gunners have different techniques, some good, some bad. Many whales will kill easily, others will fight hard for survival, but it is always a losing fight, and just means a slower death. Sometimes as many as seven harpoons are fired before the mammal dies, and it has been known for a whale to be still alive as it was held fast alongside the whaleboat. The compressed air soon finished the job—a cruel, a painful death.

Occasionally the bull sperm whale, in its last death-agony, will turn on its assailants, making for the constant thump of the propeller. Using its head as a battering-ram, it plunges directly at the turning screw. Many a catcher vessel has lost or damaged its propeller in this manner. The vessel is thrown out of commission and has to be towed to the nearest shore base for repairs or renewals.

According to many experts in the business, the most favourable conditions for chasing and killing a whale are when the mammal, on sensing the approach of a whale-boat, darts off at its utmost speed in any one direction. Whale-shooters have their own ideas on how to make a whale run the way they want. One method, used by many, is to try to overtake the whale and then put the engines Full Astern. The whirl of the displaced waters is apt to frighten the animal, and it will dart off in one direc-tion. But many whales are wily.

I liked to get our oldest whaleboat seamen—a Shetlander —talking about whale-gunners.

"Och, anybody can be a bluidy whale-shooter," he would say. "But it's anither thing to handle the boat! That's whaur the experience comes in."

He was referring to the handling of the vessel after the whale was first harpooned. The whale-line must always lead ahead, or nearly ahead, in order to keep it clear of the turning propeller. If this was not done the line was liable to whip around the screw and cause a break. The whale would be lost, the propeller might be damaged, and personnel injured.

The Shetlander went on, "By the time some of these whale-gunners are finished with a whale the puir wee thing looks like a bluidy pincushion, what with all the harpoons! What ye want is a guid angler—jist to play the whale. Aye, that's the thing—jist play the whale. He canna break onything then." He finished up by adding, "The whale-shooters mak all the bawbees. We dinna get a chance."

Most whale-gunners are temperamental and are about as superstitious as any group of Moray Firth fishermen. Their own personal failures they put down to some faulty construction of their whaleboat. Sometimes it is the harpoon gun, maybe the speed, even the propeller. It is never themselves. A comparatively poor season is explained away: "Oh, the whaleboat was no bloody good. The propeller made too much noise, you know, a singing propeller." There was always some excuse. . . .

Once our Number Four whale-shooter had had a very bad run of luck. He hadn't killed a whale in days. He started to explain about it all on radio-telephony to the whole of the Southern Ocean. The harpoon gun was no good. It never would be any good. It might as well be lying in the scrapyard and himself back home in Tönsberg. He wanted a new gun.

On board the factory vessel a brand-new gun was broken out of the cargo hold and, at great inconvenience, was mounted on the Number Four whaleboat. The old gun was taken back on board and restowed in the hold. The next day was a highly successful one for the whale-shooter and his new gun—they killed no fewer than seven fin whales. Arriving back at the factory ship that night for refuelling, he was highly pleased with himself. He was on top of the world, he had been justified.

"How is the new gun?" I inquired from the fuelling platform.

"Good, very good," he answered amicably.

But for the next four days the unfortunate man's luck again deserted him. He hadn't killed a whale in that time. He had had several *booms* (Norwegian word for failure), but no luck. With dramatic suddenness the silence of Antarctica was again shattered. The radio-telephone began to roar. He wanted the old gun back again!

And talk about being temperamental! The first time I ever saw a whale-gunner shoot at a whale it was a *boom*. He seemed to get so mad at himself that he lost all self-control. He snatched the cap from his head and threw it after the now useless harpoon. This was quickly followed by a pair of mitts and a scarf. And all the time he stamped and raved about the gun platform, using profane curses in a broad Scots dialect—his own language seemed inadequate to express his emotion.

I turned to the mate who was stationed at the helm. "What the hell's going on?" I asked. "Looks like a strip-tease act to me—or is he temperamental?"

The mate grinned. "He's temperamental all right. About fifty-fifty. Fifty per cent. temper and 50 per cent. mental. He puts on that act every time he has a miss. It seems to satisfy his personal ego, and he's all right afterwards. We like to see him that way. Besides, he keeps the ruddy slop-chest busy."

One season it was the propellers. A mediocre whale-shooter had a brilliant idea to explain away his season's poor results and lack of success. The propeller made too much noise. Within a few days all the moderately unsuccessful whale-shooters had the same excuse—their whale-boats were fitted with singing propellers. They should have been constructed not of bronze, but of stainless steel. Strange as it may seem, the owners listened. The following

Whale-factory Ship and Transport at South Georgia

Whaleboats fitting out in South Georgia

Taking off for the Search

The First Whale of the Season being
hove up the Whale-slipway

Above. The Gun Platform
of a Whaleboat

Left. A Whaleboat leaving
the Parent Vessel

A Whaleboat holding Whales

Heaving the Whale alongside

Left. Whale being harpooned

Right. Penguins on a Flagged Fin Whale being hauled alongside the Catcher Vessel

Left. A Blue Whale being towed to the Factory Ship

Right. Blue Whale on Deck

Commencing on a Blue Whale

A Whale being flensed

Above. Flensing the Blubber from
a Sperm Whale

Left. A Sperm Whale head on

Sawing up the Upper Half of the
Jaw of a Whale

Cutting up the Ribs

season all whale-catcher vessels were fitted with stainless-steel propellers. It made no difference. The mediocre whale-shooters still lagged far behind.

And there was the whale-gunner who was given chance after chance and yet failed miserably to make the grade. It wasn't because he was inactive. He did his best and worked hard enough at the job. He searched the icy ocean for long and wearying hours. But he just couldn't shoot. A bright wag from the factory vessel sent the unfortunate man a detailed plan of a new harpoon gun. It wasn't at all well received by the whale-gunner. The drawing was for a multiple pom-pom gun, which fired harpoons instead of shells!

The last thirty years have brought great changes in whale-catcher design, economy, and equipment. From the coal-burners of even the present generation the catcher has developed into a formidable oil-burning or motor-driven ship, as useful in war as in peace. It is larger, roomier, more powerful, and faster. The whale-shooter of to-day complains if his vessel cannot exceed a speed of sixteen knots.

Many modern aids have been installed. Vessels are now fitted with gyro compasses, depth recorders, radio-telephony, radio direction-finding, and radar. Marking-buoys contain automatic radio transmitters to direct the towing craft by directional bearings to their vicinity. Most of the vessels have an improved version of the war-time Asdic installation. This is an underwater rangefinder and bearing-indicator. Its function is to provide continuous information of the whale's position relative to the whale-boat during a long and exacting chase. At close range it can give warning when the whale is about to surface.

Hemp ropes have been replaced by the best Manilla and nylon. Even the harpoon has been improved, and an experimental electrical harpoon has been produced which,

when piercing the whale's body, will cause electrocution
This has not been a success because the whale-gunners
will not use them.

Notwithstanding all these modern aids and improve-
ments, the whale-gunner is certainly not happy. He seems
to think, What was good enough for my father should be
good enough for me. He killed so many whales in a season.
Why can't I do the same? Especially with all these modern
aids.

What he seems to forget is that there are not so many
whales. Twenty-five years ago a factory vessel would lie
stopped and drifting for days—even weeks. Her catcher
fleet would scour the neighbouring waters and still bring
in more whales than were required for processing. To-day
a factory ship has to be continually on the move in order
to keep up with her catcher fleet searching an ocean that
is becoming emptier and emptier of whales.

Some of the old-time whaling men have no sympathy
with modern methods. They look back nostalgically to the
free-for-all days of unrestricted whaling and fail to understand that nowadays, as whales become scarcer, international agreements are involved and the industry needs
vast outlay of capital.

"Give me back the good old days," sighed one of our old-
timers. "Why don't we forget all about these modern
ideas, forget about these gadgets, these quotas to preserve
the mammals? They will be wiped out just the same—the
sooner the better, I would say."

"What's your idea of perfect whaling conditions?" I
queried.

"Well . . . it's like this." He looked round the whaling-
deck, spat tobacco juice into the nearest open whale-
digester, and continued, "In the good old days we lay
stopped for days on end—sometimes weeks. We used to
work in the lee of a good solid ice-pack lying to the south

and running in an east–west direction for preference, with few bergs about. Clear, favourable weather, under grey or overcast skies, with an abundance of blue whales clearly visible to the naked eye. That's my idea.

"There were no quotas in those days. We took our fill and could produce just as much whale-oil as they do to-day—aye, and with only half the crew. Nowadays we have all these bloddy boffins around; all these meat-meal and oil extraction plants; chemists for the testing and grading of whale-oil, and a laboratory that is more like an operating theatre. Why, the secretary did all that work in the old days, a half-hour's job before his morning cup of tea. He didn't have any microscope or tintometer—just a few coloured slides was all the equipment he ever required.

"There were no whaling inspectors, no production officers, no biologists, not even a male nurse. We had to wash and clean the cargo tanks by hand. But we made just as much money, lived at half the cost, and paid less than half the income-tax we do to-day. Modern whaling! Bah, give me back the good old days."

I sympathized with the old-timer. Those certainly were the days. But what he did not realize was that they were gone beyond recall. The old methods would never produce enough return now. We too could stay in one place, and, for a time, we might be lucky and process plenty of whales. But it couldn't last long. Soon we should run short of whales and be forced to go off searching for them again.

12

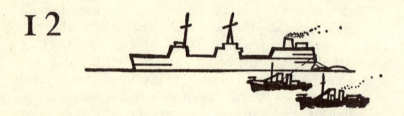

The slaughterhouse

THE first two or three weeks of whaling were always profitable if the weather was good. We usually found an area where blue whale were plentiful. Not only the factory ship was at work twenty-four hours a day—the catchers too worked round the clock, for there was little darkness. The factory vessel lay with engines stopped—drifting in the lee of some heavy ice-pack. A kick on one or other of the engines would enable the bridge watchkeepers to keep clear of any iceberg or heavy ice growler that lay directly in our path.

Catcher vessels spread out around the horizon, some in open waters, others penetrating far into the open ice lanes in search of their prey. As soon as they were fast to a whale the factory ship would be notified in code and the towing vessels were routed accordingly. They brought the dead whales back as many as a dozen at a time.

At the beginning of the season it was always an event to watch the arrival of a towing vessel. Many whalemen turned out from their watch below to inspect the load. A quick look over the whales, a mental calculation, and they could probably assess the catch down to the last barrel of whale-oil that could be processed from them. As the season wore on the event became commonplace. The towing vessel backed and filled at the stern, and the parent ship took delivery. Whales were hung off around the stern by means of hanger wires. In the meantime the whale-claw had been hove out over the slipway until it was poised just over the entry. Attached to this rumbling monster were two six-and-a-half-inch wires from the powerful steam hauling winches on 'Hell's Gate,' also two much smaller wires from two winches at the stern. A fishing-winch hove the tail of the whale into the ship by means of a four-inch wire which was rove through a system of blocks attached to buffer springs. This arrangement of spring-tension took up most of the shock and severe strains that were experienced when there were heavy seas running.

With a great thunderous clang, which was heard and felt throughout the ship, the three-ton steel claw, as if it possessed a consciousness of its own, dived upon the tail of the cadaver, and within a few seconds the dead whale was slowly mounting the slipway. The whole operation lasted for only about three minutes, but the co-ordination between the five men at the winches was truly amazing. Their movements throughout were controlled by the deck foreman. A few simple hand signals and he could make the claw behave entirely as he willed.

As the cadaver emerged and slid along the working-deck it was revealed in all its oceanic splendour. The blue whale is the largest animal known to mankind. Its length varies from seventy to one hundred feet, depending on age; its weight from seventy to one hundred and eighty tons. No words are adequate to describe the bulk of this gigantic monster of the deep—or its beauty!

As the cadaver came out of the mouth of the slipway three flensers were waiting with their knives. They made long incisions into the blubber on each side and on top as the mountain of fat was hauled slowly past them. The winches seemed to be doing most of the work. The flensers hardly moved their knifes, but each cut was deliberate and true. Flensing-wires were quickly attached to the blubber on each side of the whale, and, with spasmodic heaves, winches tore the coating of rich fat from the carcass as easily as skinning a banana. When the sides were stripped the massive jawbone was hove to the forward deck to be dealt with by the steam-driven saws. The tongue was coaxed through one of the boiler openings flush with the deck into a near-by digester. It would have been a menace to leave it lying on the open deck. It was a huge mass of slippery, jelly-like matter which took up a deck space of about sixty-four square feet.

The cadaver was now ready for turning over so that we could strip the blubber from the underside. More winches came into use. A wire was made fast to each of the whale's flukes—one over and one under the carcass. With a tremendous heave the mass was rolled completely over. It fell with a dull squelching sound, a hundred tons of meat and bone crashing to the deck. Whalemen leapt for safety, shouting, "Look out for canting!" Now the last of the blubber was stripped away, and the bloody carcass was on its way forward to be dealt with by the cutting-up gang. The whole operation was repeated aft with the next whale —and so the dis-assembly line went on.

On the forward deck lemmers and cutters began dismembering the whole of the carcass, each stroke of their knives being as true as any by a surgeon's scalpel. These men were the expert anatomists of the ship, separating flesh from bone with an ease born of years of experience. Here again, more winches tore the dismembered sections apart. Large steam saws, each with fourteen-foot toothed blades of the finest Swedish steel, were being tuned up to deal with the bone—head, ribs, jawbone, and vertebral column. Each saw was tuned to fingertip control. The head was sawn into sections small enough to pass through the mouths of the pressure boilers.

Tons of meat and in-fats were sliced from the carcass and dumped into the maws of the open digesters. The cases of ribs were hove aloft by winch and derrick, and cut into single sections. Each rib measured at least twelve feet. The innards were torn away, the huge liver separated and hove clear of the working-deck. The stomach contents and intestines were dumped overboard; all that remained was the massive backbone and back-meat. This too was quickly separated. The meat went to the dehydration plant, and the vertebral column was hove towards another bone-saw, where it was cut into small sections. It took this gang about eight minutes to dispose of the ten-ton spinal column. The gigantic butchery was over. The whale had been worked up—a bloody business! From the time the cadaver entered the slipway until nothing remained only forty minutes had passed.

Although the flensers and the lemmers were the real specialists of deck work, the cutters and the ordinary whalemen did most of the disposal work. Teams of them continuously cut and dumped blubber, meat, and bone into the huge boilers below decks. Into these went anything up to two thousand tons daily. From this huge total two thousand to three thousand barrels of pure whale-oil would be processed. In addition to this was our daily production of by-products—meat-meal, liver-meal, liver and meat extracts.

To realize the speed and skill of this work, just compare it with the time our dockers would take to discharge a bulk cargo of 2000 tons that had to be totally manhandled. On board a whaleship this amount was not only handled daily, but had to be sawn and cut up into the bargain. And we kept this up as long as our catcher fleet could supply the cadavers. Hard, bloody work.

Down in the factory spaces the scene was now vastly changed from those days on our outward voyage. Here whalemen laboured throught the twenty-four-hour day in temperatures of 110° Fahrenheit—sometimes as high as 130° in certain bottlenecks. The outside temperatures ranged from 25° to 50°, depending on the wind direction. Various ventilating systems were in use—all of them inadequate. Entering the factory during a 'full cook' was like walking into bedlam. Scores of whalemen went about their work in frenzied abandon, seemingly oblivious to anything but the job in hand. The noise and general uproar were diabolic. Electrical conveyor belts ran continuously right around the ship. Some carried the sacks of processed meat-meal in a never-ending procession from the bagging points to the cargo tanks below. Others carried bone residue from newly emptied pressure boilers directly overside into the sea.

At regular intervals the whole ship shook and vibrated as boilers were blown off to the atmosphere. Electrical motors and separators hummed. The dull thuds of vacuum pumps constantly drummed the ears. *C-l-a-n-k, c-l-a-n-k, c-l-a-n-k*, went the oil-measuring meters in a diabolic rhythm. Added to all the bustle, noise, and confusion was the powerful stench. A Hell's Cauldron indeed, manned by bedlamites by the score. One whaleman described it as "a ruddy lot of madmen working inside a big steam kettle."

Throughout the factory there was hardly room to move. To get in any direction one had to make a flying leap on to one of the bag conveyors and, in a half-crouching position, like a runner about to start for the Olympic half-mile, travel to the desired point and then take off like a champion.

I always thought I would like to see the reactions of an Inspector of Factories to this scene of mad and bewildering activity. His arms would be raised in horror—for no stranger could survive for long in this maelstrom of whirling machinery, scalding oil, and steam. There were exposed parts of moving machinery everywhere. The whalemen carried permanent bruises. The cookers, oilmen, and factory hands added to the dangers by removing the guards and safety devices from working-parts so that they could easily get at them for greasing and maintenance. They didn't bother to replace the guards until the season was over.

Along the sides of the factory gigantic, vat-like steam pressure boilers, with a capacity of about two thousand cubic feet, were in various stages of cooking out bone. Others were being filled or emptied. As soon as a boiler was cooked out and the oil run off to settling tanks, whalemen began emptying the residue to get the plant ready for another load. Time saved meant more cooking capacity. More cooking capacity meant more production. More production meant more money.

The whale-digesters were horizontal boilers with two openings to the whaling deck. Inside them was a perforated revolving drum driven by an independent motor. Steam pressure was introduced as the drum revolved. This type of boiler required no emptying: nothing remained after cooking out. In charge of the cooking, or the 'trying out,' of these whale-boilers were a group of highly skilled men. Constant care and vigilance were needed. As the contents cooked out the pure whale-oil ran off to settling tanks before going through centrifugal separators.

The separator rooms were the hottest part of the ship, where temperatures often reached 130°. The heat and humidity of these enclosed spaces where men toiled incessantly in twelve-hour shifts were appalling. They were surrounded by tanks of near-boiling oil as they worked.

The meat and liver dehydrating plants occupied another group of workers. Headed by a Scots engineer whose smile was about as bright as an Antarctic seascape, they numbered about two dozen per shift. The plants were unpopular with the whalemen, for the bonus was small, considering the hard work involved. The bagging team had a frantic race to keep up with the machines during a 'full cook.' Bags were automatically filled, but they had to be sealed and dumped on the conveyors which took them to the stowage tank. During the season at least eighty thousand sacks were used.

Whalemen had a bad habit of using these new sacks for any job that came their way. Cookers used them as cleaning rags; tradesmen used them for transporting their tools. Sacks were even used as doormats. The matter was getting out of hand. So a notice was posted up, forbidding the use of these empty sacks. It read:

DON'T TAKE SACKS

The Norwegian personnel made sure that this would be understood. Under the original notice some one had written in Norwegian:

FORBUDT TE TA SEKKER

"To hell with this!" exclaimed an angry Scot, who was well known for his nationalistic fervour and his views on Home Rule for Scotland. "These bluidy Sassenachs and Norskies, they'll soon be running the whole damned show.

Soon we'll be no be able to speak our ain language!" He seized a piece of chalk and angrily wrote:

DINNA TAK ONY BAGS

So we had it in three lingoes.

The dehydration of whale-meat has not been a great commercial success. When it was first introduced and this modern machinery installed the meat-meal was intended solely for human consumption. But it never caught on with the British public, even in the post-war years of severe meat-rationing. Frozen whale-meat could not be marketed either, and it was all sold as animal food.

This was a great pity. To whalemen, provided they do not have it served too often, whale-steak is a delicacy, and it has a nutritive value a good deal higher than beef. The mistake was to introduce to the British public whale-meat from Atlantic waters instead of from Antarctica. The whales were towed for long distances before they were processed. The result was poor-quality meat which was suspect. It did not have an earthly chance of catching the public fancy. By the time the large whaling firms offered frozen whale-meat to the market the public had been thoroughly put off. Never again will there be a chance to popularize this rich source of good meat.

Our chief butcher was an expert at preparing a whale-steak. Once a week we enjoyed our whale-steak and onions. It had to be good, because we worked in thousands of tons of the stuff all the week. Now and again some of us enjoyed a meal of whale-liver and onions. The butcher's home-made sausages were also good. He mixed whale-meat, pork, and various spices and served them at least once a week. Of course, many were revolted at the idea of eating whale in any form whatever.

"What the hell's in these bangers?" inquired one whale-man, as he poked his head into the shop one day and saw the butcher making sausages.

"Just the usual," replied the butcher. "Whale-meat and pork."

The whaleman looked around the immaculate shop and saw large heaps of whale-meat and pork, chopped up and ready to go through the mincer. "Meat and pork," he exclaimed. "I suppose you put in about fifty per cent. of each?"

The butcher grunted. "You're quite right," he said. Fifty per cent. of each. One blue whale to one pig!"

Working on a full production basis meant grinding work for the men on the factory ship. As many as sixty fin whales or thirty blue whales would be handled in twenty-four hours. Sometimes we were greedy, and the whaleboats would kill more than was necessary in case the supply ceased.

When there was a glut of whales the catcher boats were usually rationed to so many a day. We only took as many as the factory vessel could handle. Whales deteriorate rapidly after they are killed. Who was to know if the whale-shooters had a cadaver or two stowed away behind some iceberg or other, ready for the next day's operations? There was always the chance of a fog, and sometimes operational work was stopped without warning. So if a little cunning was employed no one was any the wiser, least of all the inspectors.

During these glut periods of rationed whaling the whale-meat was a problem. The meat plant could not cope with the vast quantity which lay heaped up all round the whaling deck. Many a slingful unobstrusively found its way over the side instead of into the open maws of one of the cookers—and the deck officer or the deck foreman always seemed to be looking the other way when this happened. Unless, of course, one of the inspectors was around!

At these times one could always see anything from a dozen to a score of whales moored by wires to the stern of the vessel. Gigantic blue whales, measuring about eighty to ninety feet, and fin whales only slightly smaller. Often there were sperm whales as well, but these were now a nuisance as their oil could not be mixed with the other. The monstrous cadavers, which a few hours ago had been roaming the seas as kings and queens of the ocean, looked pitiful as they floated belly up. Now they were so much dead meat, worth a few shillings to each of us whaling personnel, but thousands of pounds to the whaling interests we represented.

We used two of our whaleboats as buoyboats during these periods of heavy whaling. As the catcher or towing vessels arrived with their loads they delivered them up to the buoyboats, which held on to the cadavers until the factory vessel was ready for them. The whales, moored all round them, made the handling of the craft nearly impossible. Who cared? The factory ship was on a 'full cook,' and every one was happy.

The catcher fleet usually had caught their ration by early forenoon, and the crews were able to relax until next day's operations. Many vessels took the opportunity of coming alongside for repairs and to replenish their supplies of fuel and fresh water. Whaling equipment was loaded, the crews visited the slop-chest, and they were ready for further hunting.

Our greatest worry when on full production was fresh water. The daily consumption of fresh water for the whole expedition was about five hundred tons. This amount had to be replaced daily, or the whole works was liable to come to a standstill. When we were on full cooking capacity storage space was inadequate for large amounts. The water had to be made.

A vast evaporator plant stood in the engine-room. This could replace, or nearly replace, the enormous daily requirements. Teams of men toiled throughout the twenty-four-hour day on this operation. It was tough going, but the work has been greatly simplified of recent years by the use of various new cleaning solutions. The problem of scraping and cleaning the salt deposits from the various coils has been almost solved.

The chief engineer was always to be found by this plant if there was a shortage of fresh water. It was his greatest worry. But this presence was not appreciated by the engineer in charge of the plant and his team. This engineer once had a brilliant idea, which he thought would please his executive and maybe keep him away from the area. He chalked up on the notice-board close to the plant the following:

> MOMENT BY MOMENT
> THE WATER CREEPS AHEAD
> AS THE TIDE RUNS IN

The chief engineer was very pleased and complimented the junior on his keenness and the aptness of the quotation. "Aye, that's the way, laddie," he said pleasantly. "Give the men some encouragement in their work."

The next day some bright wag changed a couple of the words, so that the notice read:

> MOMENT BY MOMENT
> THE WATER CREEPS AWAY
> AS THE TIDE RUNS OUT

This did not go down nearly so well, and both the junior and his men got the sharp edge of the chief's tongue.

Tank storage space gave the executives another head-ache. The daily consumption of fuel-oil for the whole expedition was around two hundred and fifty tons. The production of whale-oil at full cooking capacity was five hundred tons. And as well as this extra space, space was also required for various by-products.

The old tank bosun and his tank gang worked hard at this time—sometimes for long hours far into the night. We had to keep ahead of the whale-oil production. It was all right if we had a tanker vessel in the vicinity to relieve the pressure. But we weren't always so lucky. No sooner was a fuel-oil tank emptied than it had to be got ready for whale-oil.

In the good old days, before the introduction of mechanical washers and steam jets, all tank-cleaning had to be done by hand. The usual procedure was to hang a few perforated drums of caustic at various heights throughout the tank. As the caustic melted with the introduction of live steam it was supposed to clean the tank. . . . It never did. After twenty to thirty hours of this continuous steaming the tank was opened up and had to be hosed down with near-boiling water for another ten hours. Even when this was completed considerable scraping and mopping operations had to be carried out before the tank was fit for the carriage of whale-oil. The process took about four times as long as the present method.

In those old days we had a Shetland tank bosun who was adept at the preparation of a tank. An old-timer, a proper nautical despot, he would stand over his men, zealously watching their every move. "Noo, watch yourself, mon, with that bluidy steam hose," he would shout. "Watch you dinna slip. You're no hauling the bluidy thing the right way." At frequent intervals he would dash below to the engine-room. "See here, sir, better ease that steam pressure or me men will be getting scalded."

The engineers would do their best to comply. A few minutes later he would be back. "Whit in the hell are you trying to do noo? Me men are getting frozen in the tank. Why dinna you keep the pressure up?"

The engineers go so fed up with adjusting the steam pressures that arrangements were made so that the old bosun could adjust his own pressure. There were no more complaints. The tank gang could be scalded or frozen— who cared? The old bosun was in charge of the steam pressure.

13

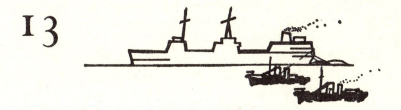

Refuelling and news from home

THE navigation bridge of the factory ship was the scene
of whirling, and sometimes bewildering, activity during
whaling days. Besides the usual navigational and watch-
keeping duties, the bridge officers were responsible for
routing the towing vessels and for the recording of all
whales killed by the catcher fleet. They were in constant
radio touch with all ships. Weather data was compiled
every four hours and radioed to the Meteorological Office,
London. A record of the ice conditions was also kept, and
ice charts had to be kept up to date. Full meteorological
equipment was carried.

The bridge seemed a world apart from the ceaseless and
bloody butchery far below. Here everything was in ship-
shape order. No passenger liner could have been more
immaculate. Brass showed up as bright as gleaming gold,
and the windows, which practically overlooked the bows

of the ship, were crystal-clear. This was all as it should be on any class of vessel—ocean liner, tramp, or even whale-factory ship.

The bridge was also a favourite place for the boffins. The doctor, the chemist, even the whaling inspectors, wandered up at frequent intervals and noted the score-card. Every whale that was killed was recorded on a black-board, and it was only a momentary job to find out the daily totals. A similar board was kept on the whaling deck for the convenience of the whalemen.

There were thousands of birds round the ship at all times. Birds of many species—from the gigantic and fascinating albatross down to the smallest snowy petrels. Thousands squatted in the water as the vessel drifted, all feeding off the organic matter that was continuously blown from the whale-cookers.

"There's old Captain Cook himself," remarked the chief chemist one day, as a huge albino albatross glided past the wing of the bridge, near enough to touch with outstretched hand. The chemist was referring to the superstition that the souls of dead seamen—even whale-men—enter into albatrosses. The old inspector, a seaman himself, gave a non-committal grunt and added, "Maybe so. But you remember this, sir, there's no seaman who does not believe in the Almighty. It's only on the bloody shore that you find men who think there's nothing greater than themselves in the universe." He waved his arms around, drawing attention to the virgin ice-pack that lay to the southward, and continued, "Man can elevate his soul to all kinds of altitudes. He may, in his own opinion, even reach the zenith. But it's no use, no use at all. It's only in these constant repetitions of nature that we can find the real, solid foundations. Foundations that lie beneath the past, the present, and the future."

It has been said that Antarctica is a preview of what

could happen if the sun ever went cold on us and the all-conquering ice smothered life. The earth would become an icy white tomb, hurtling through eternity. Even then, after all animal life had succumbed, minute flickers of living matter could still remain. We see it on the ice—microscopic plants, a form of plankton. It is edible, and it enables whales to grow to their vast bulk. I quote one of the chemists: "It is nature's elementary form of life and—who knows?—may one day be our food."

The whaling deck of a factory ship is not an ideal place to keep a biological log—but it has to be done. The gangs aft at the slipway were only concerned with the type, sex, and length of the whale. But the deck foreman, as well as the inspector, had to note all other peculiarities. Female whales must be checked for pregnancy; the length and sex of the foetus must be recorded; also the stomach contents of each whale.

Sometimes it was a frustrating job. Frequently after working up the day's catch it was found that one whale too many had been recorded, or that there was a whale missing somewhere. After a conference between the deck officer, the whaling inspector, the deck foreman, and even the ship's secretary, the discrepancy was sorted out to everyone's satisfaction—including that of the whale-gunner.

I listened one day to a slight difference of opinion between the whaling inspector and the deck foreman. It was, of course, about a whale.

"See here, bosun!" the old inspector exclaimed hotly. "That last whale you worked up—that blue whale. You've got it in the log-book as a male. It was a female. You want to be a little more careful."

The bosun grabbed the log-book. "Female!" he shouted. "If that was a bloody female, then it must have changed its sex on the way forward."

Before the War the Governments of the Falkland Islands

and the United Kingdom fitted out a vessel solely to study and mark whales in the Southern Ocean. The expeditions no doubt gathered valuable information, but the main purpose was defeated, because whales would be marked one day and the next they would be so much dead meat, blubber, and bone, having been killed by the catcher vessels of some seaborne expedition. The system was wrong. Whales were marked by shooting numbered darts made of brass into their bodies. The idea was to establish certain facts about their age and movements. But the only people who seemed to gain anything from it all were the whalemen. They received twenty shillings for the recovery of any such dart.

It was always an event when a transport tanker vessel came alongside our factory ship. It broke the monotony, and it sometimes meant mail. To the whalemen letters were few and far apart during a voyage. Invariably the first question asked by the radio officers when the tanker came within range of the radio-telephone was, "Have you any mail?" If the answer was yes a sense of wellbeing and expectation prevailed throughout the whole expedition—it meant a lot. Weather permitting, we took the tanker vessel alongside in the open sea; sometimes it was advisable, and often very necessary, to make tracks for the nearest pack-ice to get a lee. Either way it was a hazardous operation.

Three, sometimes four, whales would be used as fenders between the two vessels. They were made fast alongside the factory ship's hull at the strategic points. No fender devised by man could have been so efficient. Here were fenders weighing nearly a hundred tons each, created by nature, each with a consistency superior to the finest of rubber—safe, strong, and durable, a perfect cushion between the two vessels.

The whaleship steamed slowly ahead into the wind as

the tanker gradually came up from the stern and worked alongside. Lines were connected between the two vessels and quickly hove tight. The engines were stopped. Both ships fell off the wind, to lie drifting. Oil hoses were rapidly connected, and fuelling began. The tanker pumped fuel-oil to the whaleship and took in return whale-oil to the amount of clean tank space available. All the time whaling went on as usual.

We always had visitors from the tankers. They came on board, many with looks of amazement as they watched the bewildering activity that was going on around them. Others, from previous experience, were soon on the scrounge for sperm-whale-teeth—they usually got some. Using sperm-teeth and -bone as material, and anything from electric buffs to old razor-blades as tools, the men of the whale-factory ships spent a great part of their leisure time in carving out models and curios. Many were adept at the work and made money out of a pleasant hobby. Sperm-bone and -teeth are as hard as ivory and have a similar finish when polished. The bone is of a dull-ivory colour, with speckled streaks running through the core. Cameos, serviette-rings, lamps, book-ends, were only a few of the things turned out. More ambitious efforts were sets of chessmen, cocktail glasses, paper-weights and animal models.

Many other parts of the whale were used in this personal industry. From the baleen whale the eyeballs were made into large, translucent ashtrays. Baleen-plates or certain skin tissues could be cut out and fashioned into the most modern and futuristic lampshades. Whale-eardrums could be cut into perfect replicas of the human face. This last model, with a few deft strokes of paint, became anyting from a tough, red-bearded Scotsman to the passive countenance of a Chinese mandarin. The industry was a flourishing one.

We once had an old Shetland seaman who was a real
artist at fashioning animal models from sperm-teeth. He
specialized in penguins. He carved them swiftly and unerringly. His only tools were a few razor-blades and a small
file. One of the tanker officers was watching one day as
his quick hands filed away with frantic speed.

"I don't know how you can do it so easily," the officer
remarked.

The carver looked up and smiled. "It's verra easy, sur.
I jist look at the tooth till I can see the penguin. Then I
file awa all the bone that's over. There's nothing left but
the penguin. It's verra simple."

We usually put on a film programme for the tanker's
crew during their short stay alongside. No doubt every
ship will soon be able to show a film programme of its
own. Even ships must move with the times. Who would
have visualized, say forty years ago, that nearly every
seaman would carry around with him his own short-wave
radio receiver? It is now an essential part of a seaman's
equipment. And who would have thought that, as the
seamen went about their daily toils, the air-waves would
be filling these private radios with the trials and tribula-
tions of an atomic age?

Private radios, however, were not a success on board a
whale-factory ship. Interference was too severe. To compensate for this all B.B.C. news bulletins were recorded in
the radio-room and then relayed over loud-hailers throughout the ship. So the whalemen were kept up to date with
the latest world events.

By the time the oil tanker had delivered its fuel the
whale fenders had blown up to gigantic proportions and
the space between the two ships was jammed hard with
the intestines of whales which had been dumped from the
deck of the whaleship. Phew, what a stench! The ships
had drifted during fuelling as much as two hundred

miles. Now and then we were unlucky. If a gale came along we had to break from each other—quickly. The decisions were urgent. Every minute of delay added to the hazzards. We once rode out a westerly gale with a tanker alongside. But it was foolhardy; the tanker suffered. Both vessels drifted through large tracts of heavy pack-ice, sometimes at a speed of more than four knots. Hard, grinding blue-white ice splintered and crushed under our combined weights.

We were all glad when the fuelling and loading was done. The tanker restricted our movements, and work was apt to become disorganized. We had our mail now—to hell with the tanker! Let's get on with whaling. I well remember one dangerous incident which happened on a pre-war factory ship. We had been pumping whale-oil into a tanker vessel, and our stability was greatly affected by the enormous weight of whale we had about our decks. The vessel was top heavy. We had just hove on board one of the largest blue whales I have ever seen—a ninety-eight foot female that probably weighed one hundred and eighty tons. The cadaver had been flensed, and it was not until we started to turn it over that we ran into trouble.

Then one of the canting-wires snapped, and the gigantic cadaver took charge. Suddenly pandemonium and chaos reigned. The whale slid across the decks and struck hard against the starboard bulwarks. The slack cargo tanks of fuel-oil, whale-oil, and fresh water added to the danger. The ship heeled over to a tremendous list—well over twenty degrees away from the tanker. Mooring- and fender-wires snapped like violin strings, but the two ships held together, and damage and injury were slight. If the list had been the other way we might not have been so fortunate. The cadaver was secured and hauled gently into the centre line of the ship to bring the vessel upright.

All operations were stopped until we ballasted and brought the ship to stability . . . a narrow escape.

Whale-oil, like coconut-oil, solidifies in freezing temperatures; so it must be heated before it will pass through the pumps to the tanker. Great care must be taken to prevent overheating, as this will darken the oil and reduce its value. At last the tanker was ready to leave, having completed the first step of her homeward voyage. Soon she would be out of ice-ridden waters, with the season's first consignment of whale-oil in her tanks.

Breaking the two ships away from each other was another intricate business. Both steamed ahead to wind while the mooring-lines were disconnected. As the gap widened between them the tanker slowly forged ahead, to leave the factory ship and her whale fenders far behind.

The working-up of these fenders was a filthy and detestable job, but they were still valuable—or parts of them were. We steamed at full speed to clear some of the guts and waste that clung to them. Pitiful objects they looked now, blown up to a vast size and covered with fuel oil. And they smelt like a dozen guano factories. When they were hove on board the blubber and heads were removed. The carcasses were dumped back into the icy ocean. The whaling deck was thoroughly hosed down, in the hope of getting rid of the pervading stink which hung about for days, turning our stomachs sick.

Everything stops for Christmas

CHRISTMAS came a few weeks after the opening of the whaling season. Most of us were glad when the short festivities were over—especially the chief steward. A gigantic machine plant such as a whale-oil refinery can't be shut down just to provide everybody with a day off or a twenty-four-hour binge. Here work stopped for exactly three hours. In this interval we were provided with a stupendous meal and a bountiful supply of drinks, but we were soon back on the job. There were whales to be dealt with. Every hour the factory ship was not producing meant a loss of about £2500. Time was big money.

The catcher fleet came alongside early and collected their Christmas fare. The chief steward did them well. There were turkeys and home-fed pork, Christmas puddings and frozen fresh stawberries, as well as all the other traditional food and drinks. But the whaleboats had a day's hunting to do before they settled down to the feast.

The catering staff in the factory ship made a mighty effort. Stewards, mess-men, and boys decorated the saloons and mess-rooms with the brightest of tinsel and bunting. Christmas in Antarctica could be as cheerful as elsewhere —if only we had time to enjoy it at leisure. The three-hour break for feasting began at 5 P.M. on Christmas eve. All work stopped until 8 P.M. A skeleton gang kept the factory plant ticking over until it was time for the night gangs to go on duty.

The whalemen gathered in their respective mess-rooms, dressed respectably for the first time in months. A stranger would never realize that here were about as tough a bunch of characters as any visualized by Herman Melville. In another couple of hours they would be out again on the cold, bloody, and greasy whaling deck. And there would be no slackers. But for the moment all they were concerned about was to get down as much good food and drink as they could hold. When at last the night gang rose with a replete sigh, to change back into their filthy clothes and go back to work, the off-duty whalemen always kept the party going as long as the bottles lasted. But that wasn't long. Whalemen have a thirst like camels. When they drink they drink their fill, because they have a long, dry stretch ahead. A film programme was usually shown, but most of them were glad to get to their bunks, knowing that they would be called again at 5 A.M. for work.

Throughout these celebrations the Scots went about with dour faces. Hell! Christmas wasn't their cup of tea. It was hogmanay; and that date wasn't even recognized on a whale-factory ship—a Scottish ship at that! Never mind, they were biding their time. They all had their private bottles stowed away, religiously guarded for the correct occasion. They had their "John Haigs," their "John Grants," their "Johnnie Walkers," or whatever other 'John' was available at the last pub before sailing. They would hold their own festivities. You can't do a true Scot out of his hogmanay—it would be sacrilege. National fervour was strong among the Scots, too strong sometimes. The Shetlanders and the Borderers sometimes came to violent argument.

The Borderers regarded the island-men as blown-away Danes. The Shetlanders sneered at the Borderers as Sassenachs. In these disputes the Highland-men and the Midlanders kept strictly neutral. Yet if anyone said a word against Scotland as a whole, its customs or its peoples, the wrath of combined Caledonia would be down on him. Hogmanay had to be meticulously celebrated by them all.

One hogmanay, even though there was no recognized break from work, a few of our Scots began celebrating early, and by the time the New Year was rung in they were slightly the worse for wear. In fact, they were tight. One red-bearded native of the Hebrides began his usual practice of baiting the Sassenachs.

"Why the hell don't you shut up?" said an aggressive whaleman from the county of Durham. "You know what's the matter with you bloody people? You're all the same. You're not satisfied to stay in your own country —you have to go out and around, sticking your noses in other people's affairs. It's the same the whole world over, whatever the country. You Scots have to go and organize the bloody place. Why the hell don't you all stay at home?"

The red-bearded Scotsman listened to this angry outburst from his Tyneside shipmate. He even sobered up a little. "Aye—maybe you're right," he said. "But you canna blame the Scots all of the time. Hell! There's a wee village in Scotland and all the bloody inhabitants are Sassenachs—about 90 per cent. of them, anyway. What do you say about that?"

The Tynesider looked around as if for moral support, but he was outnumbered by about twenty to one. He shrugged and said, "Never heard of the place. I just don't believe it."

"No? Then let me tell you it's just a tiny wee place by the name of Bannockburn! Heard of it now? It's overpopulated by Sassenachs all right. But they're all under the bloody ground!"

The Geordie whaleman was getting annoyed "Give it a rest," he said. "You're just like a bloody fog-horn—nothing much to look at, but you make a hell of a noise. Why don't you go back to your own country and forget to come away again?"

The situation was becoming tense, and a battle seemed likely, when a fellow-Scot barged his way through the hostile crowd gathered round the unfortunate Englishman. "Now, then." he said gruffly. "Dinna be like the bloody whale. The only time he gets into danger is when he starts to spout." He grabbed the Sassenach, there was a dull *plunk*, and the whaleman went down as if he had been harpooned. "Aye, that's right—Bannockburn," the Scot murmured reverently.

One of the best Christmases I ever spent away from home was on the island of South Georgia. Here there was no mad rush to get the festivities over, and preparation was made days before. The catcher vessels were ordered to spend Christmas in port, and the whole station looked forward to the celebrations.

A friendly gesture was first made by decorating the service boat with flags and bunting and sending her, under the command of her old skipper, to the Government post at Grytviken. The skipper, masquerading as Father Christmas, in a costume that would have done credit to any departmental store's Toyland, went round issuing presents and delicacies to the Government officials and their families. Toys, made by various tradesmen, were presented to the post's few children.

The service boat's crew were well received. First they visited the magistrate's house, then on to the customs- and police-officers, in that order, and finally to the Government radio-officers. When it was time to return to the whaling station every one was in a merry mood. There too they had started celebrating early. At this shore station work ceased at 4 P.M. on Christmas eve, and about four hundred whale-men settled down to a twenty-four-hour holiday—the only stoppage of work in the whole year. The dinner on Christmas eve was a huge success. There was a bountiful supply of drinks, and after the feasting the whalemen all settled down to their own little parties—here, there, and everywhere. These lasted well into the early hours of Christmas morning. Piano-accordion players made the rounds of the mess-rooms to lead the singing of Christmas carols and Norwegian and Scottish folk-songs. It was late on Christmas Day when the whale-gunners took their vessels to sea again. The hunting and killing of whales had to go on in spite of their thick heads.

Mid-season was the medical officer's busiest time on the factory ship and in the catcher vessels. Broken limbs and mangled hands were commonplace. There were also the usual minor ailments, but colds and influenza are almost non-existent in the Antarctic climate—unless we had a tanker alongside to bring us a supply of germs. It was a curious fact that as soon as a transport vessel was alongside, especially if she came direct from the United Kingdom, an epidemic of some kind was almost sure to break out among the whalemen.

Most seasons there was at least one major accident—usually in a catcher ship. A whaleman on deck when a whale had been harpooned and the line was racing out at terrific speed could get tangled in the line. A limb might be mangled or even severed. It was then a hell of a job for the doc—especially in bad weather when trans-shipment was nearly impossible. Getting to the injured seaman in heavy seas was no easy job in itself. Then he had to do a surgical operation on board the bucking whaleboat—a feat nearly as difficult as threading a needle on the back of a show-jumping horse.

One of the doctor's worries was coping with whalemen who become neurotic. The monotony of a whaling voyage with its endless repetition of twelve-hour shifts sometimes produced an environment of discouragement and frustration. A touch of emotional disturbance is common even to the best of us. It can be stimulating, even valuable, to a well-balanced character. But too much of it can be completely ruinous. The doctor had to show real understanding, plus a sense of humour, and this combination often brought this serious ailment into focus. The ship's executives were generally taken into consultation about treatment, for a neurotic whaleman was a problem to us all.

We once had a doctor who was a fresh-air fanatic. His daily rig, close to the Antarctic Circle, was more suitable for the Congo—khaki shirt and shorts. Whether this was sheer bravado or complete foolishness we never discovered. Entering the surgery, the hospital, or even his own cabin, was like going into a refrigerated chamber. All ports and doors were permanently open to the glacial breezes of Antarctica. He was almost a vegetarian, and his pet theory was that vitamin pills were the cure for all ailments. He believed that Captain Cook, the great British seaman and navigator, was about one hundred and fifty years ahead of his time. He explained that there was never any scurvy or beriberi among Captain Cook's crews because he insisted that his seamen ate various seaweeds and the offal of seals and other marine life. Of course, Cook did not know about vitamins, but he seemed to know what was necessary to health. Our doctor thought *he* knew too, and he applied his knowledge with ruthless despotism. He would diagnose a patient's complaint in a matter of seconds, hand him a couple of vitamin pills, with possibly a purgative for good measure, deliver a short lecture on the uses and value of vitamins—and the ailing whaleman would find himself on the other side of the surgery door, with the pills in his hand and with no alternative but to go back to work on the whaling-deck.

One way we combated monotony aboard was to issue a grog ration on Saturday night. All whalemen were given a tot of rum, and it was a welcome event in a week of never-ending grind. The only trouble with rum is that it makes a new man out of you, and consequently the first thing the new man wants is another drink. Most whalemen take water with their spirits—about half-and-half. But they like plenty of water when it has rum in it, so on Saturday nights a few of the off-duty boys would get into a happy mood. They felt they had earned it. And another week had gone by. Roll on the end of the whaling season!

15

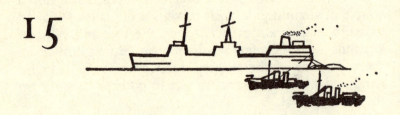

Killer whales and penguins

IN the sullen, ice-strewn seas of Antarctica the harpooned whales, after their desperate struggle with man, lie silent and awash. In death they are like islands of flesh, like upturned ships abandoned to the waves.

But from the huge cadavers all is not silent. Embedded in the blubber there may be radio marking-buoys, automatically transmitting a signal over the wastes of ocean. It is weird and uncanny to hear from far off these signals from the deep which enable the towing craft to steer unerringly towards them. So the spoils of whaling are collected and brought back to the mother ship, often as many as a dozen in one haul.

But many of the whale-catchers are in too much hurry to leave the radio buoys behind them at the scene of a kill. The buoys take time to fix. They are often too eager for the next kill to wait for the buoys to be fitted up.

A quicker method is to stick a flag-spear into the whale. This is a long bamboo pole which carries the whale-shooter's pennant and a number for all to see. A distinguishing mark is cut into the cadaver's tail as an additional safeguard. In the darkest days of the season a small electric light is also fixed to the spear, to signal across the sea. When the gunner reports a kill directional bearings are exchanged between his ship and the factory vessel. Then it is the turn of the towing vessels.

Life aboard these ships is much more orderly and sedate than in the killer fleet. Their job is not so spectacular and exciting, but it is just as interesting and educational.

Towing vessels for seaborne expeditions came into use just after the Second World War. They were all Flower Class corvettes, converted at great expense to the uses of whaling. Each had spent a short but useful life as a unit of the Royal Navy during the war years. As corvettes they fought through the Battle of the Atlantic, and they did stout work on the convey route to Murmansk. Each vessel had a history of courage and heroism by the men who manned it in the fight against the Nazi U-boat. To-day these ships go about their peaceful work—if you can call whaling peaceful. They are valuable units to all pelagic expeditions. Hunting U-boats and hunting whales have something in common.

Sometimes the supply of whales in the area we were working fell off. One of the towing vessels would be sent away on a long scouting expedition to look for a better place. If the scout ship reported plenty of whales the whole fleet steamed at full speed towards this area. Slack periods meant little work for towing craft, but when whaling was in full swing theirs was a night-and-day grind. There is time and opportunity aboard a towing vessel to observe the Antarctic seascape and its marine life. The crews are not obsessed with the frenzy of killing and processing the whales. Steaming through broken-up ice-packs can prove as interesting as a walk through a country lane in early spring. Stretching to infinity is the white, virgin ice. Blue avenues of ocean, lined with blue-white icebergs, open up ahead of us. Farther and farther to the southward the ice forms into a compact, frozen mass. Variable winds and currents cause it to pile up and telescope into fantastic shapes. Ridges form, sometimes as high as twenty feet.

From a towing vessel you have a chance to observe the most voracious, the most cunning, the most dangerous, of all Southern Ocean mammals—the killer whale. They are the scavengers of the ocean, who hunt in packs like wolves. They are about thirty feet long and are as remorseless as vultures. A large pack of them will even attack the living blue whale. But dead whales are much easier prey, and the killers constantly follow the whaleships, feeding off the offals and tearing out the tongues of the whales as they lie moored at the stern. They approach silently, with only a swirl of displaced water as they break surface to breathe. But their fearsome, triangular fins stand about five feet out of the water. Their loathsome, cavernous mouths are much fiercer than the sharks' and about five times larger. Within seconds they are among the dead whales, like vultures feeding on carrion. Large masses of blubber and tongue are torn away from the cadavers, and the killers make off. But they will be back if they dare. Rifles are always kept at the stern to fight them off. A few well-directed shots into the bodies of the leaders quickly turn the whole pod around. The uninjured killers now turn and devour their crippled companions.

Another voracious killer is the sea-leopard. He is about twelve feet long and fur-coated. To me he always looked like the incarnation of evil. His skin is valuable and useful for many purposes, but he is too difficult to kill for hunting him to be a business proposition. Experienced whalemen are more wary of sea-leopards than of any other animal of the Southern Ocean. They will attempt to capsize any small boat and will attack a human on land as well as in water.

The Adélie penguins are funny little fellows, With their black coats, white waistcoats, and webbed red feet, they waddle and strut about on the ice floes with arrogance and bravado, as if the whole of Antarctica was their own private property. They have no fear—except for the sea-leopard. Watch a group of penguins on the edge of an ice-floe and about to enter the water: they will push the smallest among them into the water first to find out if it is safe for the rest. The sea-leopard often lies in wait beneath an ice-floe and will snap up the poor little Adélie. But if the trial penguin survives the test the rest of the flock are quickly seaborne.

I once watched a football match between two teams of whalemen in South Georgia at which the spectators were a crowd of our seamen and a group of about a hundred penguins. The penguins seemed as interested in the play as the humans. Every time the ball was kicked in their direction they moved back collectively and just out of range. As soon as play moved to another part of the field the penguins surged forward again. Their natural curiosity about human beings lures them frequently within arm's length—but just you try to catch one! They waddle and slide until they reach the ice, then they are speedier than a toboggan. In the water they are greased lightning.

The penguin family are happy, contented, and seem to thrive in captivity. They are favourites in all zoological gardens, both with the young and the not-so-young. We once shipped sixty penguins from South Georgia for the London and Edinburgh zoos. They ranged from the majestic Emperor to the tiny Adélie. All were beautiful specimens. They had been captured around the coast, and it had been a long and strenuous job to collect them, not because penguins were scarce, but because only the best were wanted. A pen was built for them in the whale-slipway. We hove them on board in home-made wooden crates. On the deck of the factory ship they surveyed their surroundings with great curiosity. Then, with a waddling walk like whalemen home after a long voyage, they marched to their new home.

All went well with our prize passengers until we reached the tropics. Then they began to show signs of fatigue and distress. We provided them with running water in large troughs, but it was not enough. So our plumbers rigged up a system of overhead perforated pipes and connected them up to the sea service-line. Below the pipes we installed a canvas pool so that the penguins could live in a perpetual shower-bath. That suited them fine. It was amusing to watch their antics in the cooling waters. At meal-times there were always crowds of seamen watching them being fed. Fish was their only diet. "The darn things are better fed than we are," one sailor said. They all survived the difficult voyage to the United Kingdom, and I suppose they have since provided many happy and amusing hours for multitudes of people.

Occasionally one of the little Adélies came aboard the factory ship when we were whaling. He would waddle up the whale-slipway and look round like a tipsy old man in evening dress. You could almost be sure there was something wrong with him. It is a curious fact that the penguin seems to know he will receive help from the human if he is in trouble. I particularly remember seeing one lonely, pathetic little figure standing at the top of the slipway, looking dejectedly around him. From head to foot he was covered in a thick coating of fuel-oil which, no doubt, had come from one of our catcher vessels.

I watched two of the flensers give the penguin first aid.

First they wiped the poor little fellow down with paraffin, taking care that it did not go into his eyes. Then they washed him thoroughly with soap-suds for about ten minutes. Finally they lightly hosed him with salt water. From the miserable object of half an hour before he now emerged an immaculate figure. He triumphantly looked over his gleaming black-and-white coat and glanced solemnly around him as if to express his appreciation. Then with a slow but impressive waddle he reached the head of the whale-slipway, and *w-o-o-s-h!* he was gone!

At mating-time multitudes of penguins appear out of the ice waters of Antarctica. They gather on the rocky coasts of the Southern Ocean islands to hatch and rear their young. The whalemen often raid their rookeries and steal as many as two thousand eggs at one outing. Once I went with a raiding party. The nests are always high on some rocky headland. As you climb up you are assailed by the overpowering stench of their droppings, which lie thick on the foreshore and on every rock and ledge. Then you come upon a wild landscape dotted by thousands of penguins, silently squatting with their eggs between their feet. These patient, absorbed creatures, oblivious to wind and cold and the loneliness of nature, are a moving and fascinating sight.

But the rough whalemen are in no mood to study the habits of the penguin colony. Brutally they stride among them, poking the birds out of the way. Behind them come a gang collecting the eggs. The penguins break their silence with loud shrieks of "*C-a-ak! C-a-ak!*" They assume a fierce expression and try to peck the raiders' legs. But the whalemen can safely ignore them. Their knee-length leather boots protect them from the rage of the poor penguins.

16

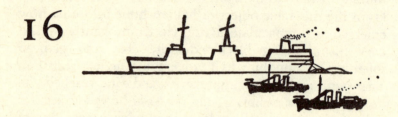

Southern Ocean gale

As the season wore on the darker and longer nights closed in around us. Whale-catcher vessels now had to go much farther afield in their unrelenting hunt for whales. Towing craft had long, wearying tows back to the factory ship. At this stage of the season most of the dead whales were delivered in the night hours.

If you looked down by night from the aft end of the navigation bridge the whaling deck was a weird and gory sight. Huge arc lights at all strategic points about the superstructure shone down on the blood-spattered deck. Whales—as many as four at one time—were in various stages of being dismembered. Great mountains of blubber, meat, and bone, in brilliant hues of white, red, and pink, were heaped as high as the bulwarks. Man looked puny and insignificant alongside these gigantic cadavers.

During the latter half of the season gales were frequent.

Sometimes we were caught in one with as many as fifty whales to work up. Then every man of the fleet faced an ordeal. In such an emergency catcher vessels were responsible for their own dead whales until the factory ship could take delivery.

The Antarctic gale comes up suddenly. Sometimes a rapidly falling barometer or a grotesquely beautiful sunset is the only indication of the gathering storm. The catcher fleet would then race for the shelter of the nearest ice—if there was any near. They towed their dead whales with them. Frequently the whole expedition was caught in a gale with no chance of shelter. Then all hell was loose. The wind began with an ominous moan, and the skies became leaden and formidable. At first there was a short, rolling sea. This quickly changed to a boiling white-and-grey mass, making it difficult to distinguish where sea ended and sky began. To add to the hazards of Nature's fury, scores, often hundreds, of icebergs drifted around us. Many of them calved in the storm and split into granite-like growlers of blue ice which tossed about in the boiling ocean.

Catcher vessels that found the leeward side of some large iceberg were in a place of unnatural calm and stillness in an ocean of chaos and disorder. Many vessels, unable to make shelter, paid out their dead whales on the end of a heavy wire, and lay to this efficient sea-anchor as supplied by nature. They rode out a gale in this fashion, but all held on fanatically to their whales, whatever the cost.

On board the factory vessel there was no let-up in spite of the weather until the last cadaver was worked up. We lay in the trough of the sea, drifting to a broadside of mountainous waves and shrieking wind. We could not heave to without shutting down the whole of the production processes. This was done only in the greatest emergency.

On the decks whalemen laboured in a slithering mass of greasy blubber, slimy meat, and bone. Flying spume and icy spray, mixing with the coagulated blood, quickly froze to everything—even to their beards. They cursed their unhappy lot, but they worked with the usual enthusiasm and abandon. Weather was all in the day's work. The job was to get these whales worked up before they rotted. The deck foreman, with profane but kindly encouragement, helped those in difficulty. For the flensing gangs work in this weather was nerve-racking. The screaming maelstrom forced heavy seas to sweep up the whale-slipway when, perhaps, there was a 100-ton cadaver being hauled up, suspended only by the two great wires that were shackled to the whale-claw. Sometimes we lost one. The whale was perhaps half-way up the slipway when an already damaged tail broke with a sharp crack like that of a large gun. The three-ton claw flew through the air, empty. And the whale slipped back into the sea, to be lost in the turbulent waters.

Delivering whales to the factory ship in this weather required seamanship and perseverance of the highest order. As the whale-shooter manœuvred at the stern his vessel was sometimes high in the air on the crest of a wave and the next moment far below us in the trough. It was a fearsome job. As each whale was hove into the slipway angry seas carried it far up the incline. Next moment the winchman was slacking away madly as the stern lifted and left a single wire holding the entire weight of the cadaver. This was when the spring-tensioned blocks came into action. Without these buffer springs the job would have been impossible.

The deck foreman watched warily for his chance to grab the next whale. Two or more successive high seas and then a lull. Here was a chance. Down dropped the whale-claw with a thunderous clang, and the whale rapidly came up the slipway. But sometimes the foreman was unlucky, and the whale, the claw, and the wires were tangled up in an unholy mess. It all had to be sorted out. Whale after whale was made fast on deck, until every one was delivered. Then the catcher skipper, with a sigh of relief, made off towards shelter, unburdened by his cumbersome load, and another whaleboat began the same struggle to get his whales aboard.

Down in the factory spaces there was always trouble during foul weather. Conveyor belts leading overboard had to be stopped, and all openings were sealed. It was impossible to empty the bone residue from the pressure boilers, so they were refilled and cooked out a second time. The tossing of the ship sent loose material rolling around. The deck machinery groaned under excessive strains. And so did the men.

On the navigation bridges the expedition's manager and his navigating officers spent an anxious time while the gale lasted. Visibility was almost nil, and they were at a great disadvantage because they did not have a full-powered vessel under their control. All steam power was required for the production of whale-oil and by-products.

As the ship drifted engines were used only to avoid the icebergs which lay directly in our path. Radar then proved its tremendous value to us. Without it we could not have survived. In twenty-four hours the factory vessel might drift well over a hundred miles. Ice conditions changed so rapidly that at sunset there might be only a few bergs near us, yet by dawn there might be hundreds. We could rely on our all-seeing eye to save us from disaster.

Luckily, Antarctic gales subside as quickly as they spring up. Within a few hours there may be scarcely a ripple on the water. This sudden subsidence is due to the large areas of solid pack-ice that lie to the southward and to the near-freezing temperature of the water. The moment the gale had begun to die down towing boats were quickly off the mark, scouring the waters to windward, searching for whales which were lost from the factory vessel during the storm. They were picked up and towed back to be processed.

But sometimes days passed when we had no whales to work on—days of fog and quietness; no rumbling noises from the whale-claw or from the deck winches; no violent hissing of steam as whale-boilers were blown. Factory ship and her brood of catchers lay quiet and drifting while radar probed the blinding mists, seeking out the hidden ice dangers.

A regular and severe routine of duties was carried out during fog or bad weather. Maritime routine, in its essential details, varies little in any ship, whatever the nationality. Whaleships are no exception. Cleaning and routine duties were always found, not only for their own sake, but also to prevent too much leisure and consequently the brooding over such a wearisome life. The furnace-hot factory spaces became as cold as the icebergs which were for ever drifting by. Then the whalemen went about their duties with dour, glum faces. They were days when we made no money—days of gloom.

On foggy days the most enterprising of the whale-shooters steamed their vessels for long distances in an attempt to find clear weather. They sometimes succeeded and enabled us to get an extra whale or two. In the factory, meanwhile, we had the gear and machinery to overhaul, accommodation spaces to clean, and a hundred and one duties that could only be done at this time. Throughout the season large piles of baleen mounted up. Now was our chance to clean and dry this whalebone. The baleen-plates were scrubbed in soapy water and then hung up to dry. They were bagged and stowed in a dry place. There was money and a market still available for this product of a bygone era.

From whaling to soap-making may seem a far cry, but it is a switch that often happens on whaleships, where soap is used in quantity. Now and again, during slack times, we turned out a batch of soap. An eighty-gallon steel drum fitted with suitable steel coils was used as a boiler. The ingredients—whale-oil, resin, and some caustic soda— were introduced in their proper quantities and a small amount of salt water added. After four hours of very slow boiling the salt water was run off and the now manu- factured soap poured into five-gallon drums and allowed to solidify.

One gang thought this soap-making job was too easy, too monotonous. "To hell with this yellow soap," said one bright whaleman. "Let's have a go at making some car- bolic." The batch of carbolic soap, even if not up to the standards of the best "Lifebuoy," turned out fairly well. But the stock of carbolic deodorants from the ship's store was wiped out in the process. It was a good job we carried no perfumes. I always thought that this soap-making was an expensive economy.

Now was the time for hobbies to while away the slack days. The whalemen got out some of their stored sperm- whale-teeth and worked away with hand-file, razor-blades, and sand-paper. Watching them carve animal models, cameos, and other intricate articles was an education. No electric buffs were required. Everything was done by hand, and every one had his own ideas of how best to go about the business. Competition was keen. Even the tradesmen had the bug. Besides the use of sperm-bone and -teeth, various materials—wood, brass, copper, and steel—were often used. One tradesman was noted for his skill in repro- ducing to scale a perfect working-model of the harpoon gun.

We were steaming all the time during these times when whales were scarce. Our catcher fleet would be out ahead of us in fan-shaped formation. As soon as whales were sighted bearings were exchanged, and all ships sped in that direction. One of our senior gunners was usually sent away on a scouting expedition to prospect for whales. He would penetrate far into the ice, looking for open water beyond. It was often a dangerous job, but we never had a case where the catcher vessel was unable to extricate herself from these vast areas of ice. A lane could always be found leading outward, and more often than not this would be to the north-west. 'When in doubt steer to the north-westward' seemed to be the safest procedure, probably because the prevailing currents opened up the ice in this direction.

The whale-shooter would stop his vessel during the dark hours in case he overlooked a good whaling area. It was queer lying there, a small ship in the midst of a wilderness of ice. The unnatural stillness tried the nerves of anyone who experienced it for the first time.

Many landsmen who use the expression 'She makes heavy weather of it' do not realize what it means to a seafarer. He often uses it to refer to an awkward or an unlucky ship. Only when there is a calm sea are these unfortunate and unhappy ships comfortable. Even in a moderate sea they pitch and roll violently, creaking and groaning in every rivet. They climb a swell as if climbing to the sky, then fall into a trough of sea as if seeking rest in the ocean deeps. A hoodoo is on them—they are unlucky and always in trouble.

Other ships make good weather of it. A storm to them seems only a moderate breeze; a confused sea a mere ripple. They are the lucky ships. It isn't the fault of the men who sail in an unlucky ship. A change of crew makes little or no difference. There will always be lucky and unlucky ships. Whale-factory ships and their attendant

vessels are no exception. There are the lucky and the unlucky ones. Let me give you an example.

Number Three whaleboat was a comparatively new
ship. As a modern whale-catcher vessel she was all that
could be desired, well built, highly powered, a ship to
inspire confidence in all who saw her for the first time.
But to the whalemen who had to operate her—she was
the last thing in hoodoo ships. Nothing went right with
her; she spent considerable time alongside the factory ship
for repairs and engine adjustments; she lagged far behind
her sister ships in the number of whales killed during a
season. This had gone on ever since she had come out new.
Then a new whale-shooter was appointed to Number
three whaleboat. Somehow he and his crew brought a
new look to this vessel. She was now efficient where
previously she had been mediocre. The crew were happy.
They had laid the hoodoo—or so they thought. They were
running neck-and-neck for the leading position.

One morning Number Three catcher vessel delivered
up to the factory ship two large blue whales. She then
made off to the southward to resume hunting. At 4 P.M.
the same day the factory vessel could not establish radio-
communication with Number Three. This was not unusual,
as many whale-shooters failed to keep the schedule if they
were in the act of chasing or killing a whale. Again at 8 P.M.
the catcher vessel failed to answer repeated signals from
the factory ship. This was attributed to radio-transmitting
trouble, again not unusual in catcher vessels.

In the early dawn of the next day Number Five whaleboat sighted an unfamiliar object on the distant horizon.
She sped to investigate. As the whaleboat closed the bearing
the object was revealed as a flooded lifeboat. Something
was very wrong. In the lifeboat were eight dead men and
one young boy, unconscious. The lifeboat bore the name
of Number Three whaleboat.

Communication was instantly established with the factory vessel. The sea was searched over a wide area by the whole catcher fleet. But there were no other signs. The boy recovered rapidly, and his story, although incoherent in places, added up to this:

In the late afternoon the catcher vessel sighted a large blue whale and gave chase. This whale had been hunted before and knew all the answers. Every time it sounded it came up on another bearing. The whale-shooter made repeated attempts to get within range for a shot, but never succeeded. After about ninety minutes of futile chasing the whale suddenly surfaced close under the bow, too close for the whale-shooter to bring the gun to bear. The order was given to put the helm hard over to starboard. The vessel heeled over to the change of helm, continued heeling, and capsized with engines racing at full speed.

The crew had no chance. Many were trapped inside the vessel. Others were swept into the icy seas. One flooded lifeboat floated away from the ship. Some of the crew got into it, but they died from exposure in the bitter Antarctic night. Out of a happy and gallant crew of seventeen the boy was the only survivor.

Although many of the old dangers of whaling have long since been eliminated by the uses of modern aids, just as many dangers have been added. Whale-gunners now have to take far greater chances in an ocean where there are fewer and fewer whales. The averages must be kept up, otherwise the job is not worth the risks, or the hardships, or the continuous grind of a monotonous environment. True, whale-catcher ships have become larger and now have better amenities, but these do not make up for the continuous struggle against nature in her worst moods. There is no such things as comfort aboard a whale-catcher.

Talk about taking chances! A well-known whale-shooter once got fast to a large blue bull whale that showed great fight. The line had been allowed to run out until there was nearly three-quarters of a mile of six-inch Manilla rope trailing behind the mammal. The brakes were slowly applied, and the catcher lay to a rigid line with the whale still fighting. Slowly but surely it was hove back as the huge steam winch reeled in.

The gunner waited on his platform, ready to send another harpoon into the madly fighting whale, when the bull's mate turned in her flight and surfaced close on the starboard bow. The gunner could not resist the temptation. *B-O-O-M!* The harpoon gun roared. The second harpoon buried itself in the female whale. The line screamed from the other locker, and the gunner and his crew now had two madly fighting blue whales straining at the bow leads.

How would you like to tackle a couple of big salmon, hooked by rod and reel held one in each hand? Such a task was child's play concerned with the gunner's dilemma. The job seemed impossible. Yet he landed his whales.

One season the same gunner was in more serious trouble. Chasing a small pod of fin whales, he wanted to head them off quickly. The shortest route was between two icebergs that lay a short distance apart. He sent his whaleboat at full racing speed between the two bergs. *C-R-A-S-H!* The vessel brought up with a buckling noise as the stem below the waterline struck solid ice. The ship shuddered and heeled over at an alarming angle. The engine-room and boiler spaces were flooded. There were a few seconds of pandemonium and chaos, during which one of the engineers managed to shut off all steam pressure before he escaped from the engine-room. A terrible silence followed. The vessel slid off an underwater ice shelf and slowly righted herself. Disabled and a major repair job, she was towed to South Georgia.

Many and varied are the repairs done to the catcher fleet during the short season. Whaleboats must be kept in commission at all costs. As soon as a defect is noted the vessel is brought alongside the factory ship at once—generally with a whale between them as a fender. A squad of tradesmen go on board. Then there are no stoppages, no meal intervals, until the repair is done, however long it takes. The chief engineer of the factory vessel supervises the work, and all whaleboat engineers come under his sole direction.

Whale-factory ships also have their troubles, although accidents are now very rare because of radar. Instead of groping through the blinding mists, the watchkeepers now know exactly where the hidden ice dangers lie. To-day we travel at full speed if necessary through the thickest of fogs, relying solely on radar to tell us the perils forty miles away.

Before the War factory vessels drifted blindly through fog and darkness. Their only safeguard was to place a whaleboat on the lee side to patrol the area. A pre-war factory vessel in which I served once had a narrow escape. We were late in getting South that year because of a delayed sailing and adverse weather. Approaching South Georgia and well behind our schedule, we were held up by large areas of fog. Risks had to be taken if we were to begin whaling at the proper time. The vessel was kept at a moderate speed. Look-outs were doubled and all possible precautions taken. But what is a moderate speed when you have no radar and are surrounded by ice? Suddenly, what we dreaded happened. Out of the greyish blackness loomed a gigantic white blur, an iceberg. The engines were instantly put Full Astern. But with a jarring crash the whaleship buried her nose in the ice mass. Look-out men scampered for their lives as hundreds of tons of granite-like ice crashed on the foredeck.

Our strong and worthy vessel looked sorry for herself. The stem was buckled back a distance of sixteen feet. The steam windlass was smashed, and we had left our port anchor and forty-five fathoms of chain cable buried somewhere inside the frozen mass. The forepeak was buckled, and the heavy steel frames and girders, which provided structural strength, were now a conglomeration of twisted steel. Still, they had done their job—the collision bulkhead was intact.

On arrival in South Georgia there began a frantic race to get our vessel seaworthy and fit to face the rigours of an Antarctic whaling season. Scores of men were employed on the non-stop job. Twisted steel was burned away, and a gigantic cement box was built within the forepeak to compensate for the loss of structural strength.

The vessel sailed on time, and better still—we completed a record season.

17

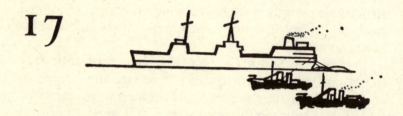

Encounter with an iceberg

THE season was nearly over. We now had to cover vast distances in our search for whales. From the South Orkneys to the Weddell Sea we had hunted, sometimes with success, sometimes with disappointment. We always seemed to complete a whaling season somewhere round the South Shetlands. Fin whales were always numerous in this area, but they were of a much smaller species. We made up for this by the numbers we caught. Sometimes our daily haul would exceed sixty. Against this, we often had periods of fog, gales, and severe ice conditions which restricted our output.

Elephant and Clarence Islands stand at the entrance to Bransfield Strait. From the sea they look much the same as the massive islands of floating ice that continuously drift about the South Shetlands. It was from Elephant Island that Sir Ernest Shackleton started on one of the greatest open-boat voyages in the history of mankind—an epic of human endurance that will live for ever in the annals of Antarctica.

We were now nearing our expedition's quota. But how long would the units last out? Were the other expeditions as successful as we were—or had they done better? Our quota for by-products had long been passed, and we were now on an increased bonus rate. This individual quota system, arranged by the whaling firms themselves, takes an unfair advantage of the whaleman. It means that the quota set is the average production of the last three seasons—not a very satisfactory way of repaying successful endeavour.

We were constantly on the move during the last two weeks of the season, trying to keep up with fast-moving whales. We often sighted other pelagic expeditions using the same techniques. We quickly separated, as if by mutual consent. News, or whaling information, was never exchanged. Indeed, the subject of whaling was taboo, unless one or the other tried a form of bluff.

End-of-season conditions were deplorable. We had tolerable days, but gales were habitual, and we were constantly in open water with heavy swell at all times. Whaleboats were often unable to get alongside, and refuelling had to be carried out from the stern with both vessels under way. Darkness set in by 4 P.M.; the Southern winter was approaching. Seals and penguins were scarce—and so were whales. Birds—millions of them—seemed to be gorging themselves for the last time before setting off on their long migrations. In the dark their snow-white bodies looked like monstrous snow-flakes by the rays of the deck searchlights.

Morale was never good at this time. "Hell, I wish it was all over," "What a bloody life," "No more of this game for me—it's back to the trawlers when I get home," were typical remarks. But as long as there are whales there will always be whalemen.

On board the whaleship it was easy to distinguish men and their various jobs. The deck crowd, the flensers, the cutters, and the deck labourers looked tanned and weather-beaten, while the factory squad were haggard and sallow-looking. However, one or two weeks in the open air soon brought them back to normal.

We had got rid of our last tanker vessel and now retained only sufficient oil fuel to complete the season and return to South Georgia. At this time 30 per cent. of our tank storage space was taken up with by-products. We never transferred these to transport ships.

As our total fuel consumption was roughly two hundred and fifty tons daily for the expedition, organization had to be good to meet the necessary requirements. One season—the first year of World War II—it was not so good and nearly lost us a whale-factory ship.

Several days previously we had taken delivery of our last fuel for the season. Unfortunately, the oil contained a large quantity of water and sludge, the scrapings from the oil storage tanks at South Georgia. It seemed all right, especially as the water was being drained off at the settling tanks before the oil was used. The engineers were happy, and so were we all. We were on full cooking capacity.

Calamity struck one forenoon. We were heaving a cadaver on board, when a shout went up that there was insufficient steam. Within a few minutes the whole ship went dead. Steam petered out from both winches and cookers. Electrical lights and motors went off as the steam generators failed. Sludge had been pumped to the furnaces.

Lying to leeward, immediately in our drift, were several barrier icebergs. There were no catcher vessels in the vicinity, and radio and telephony transmitters were un-workable. We couldn't even summon help. A squad of a hundred men or more immediately organized into a working-party. Armed with buckets of diesel oil taken

from the galley fuel tanks, they formed a chain-gang to
pour the Diesel oil from a height, in the form of a gravity
system, to the boiler furnaces below. The fires were re-
lighted, but still there was no steam.

Gradually we crept nearer to the icebergs. We had
hauled about a dozen whales from aft and brought them
along the ship's side to act as a buffer; but no buffer, whatever its construction, could withstand thousands of tons
of granite-hard ice. The nearest berg was within six hundred
feet of us, and disaster seemed imminent, when one of
those miracles which only nature's elements can perform
happened. The wind shifted. The factory vessel swung
slightly and altered her drift approximately eight points.
We were saved. Instead of having the nearest iceberg
abeam, we now had it astern. It was awesome standing
there at the stern watching the towering ice mass as we
slowly drifted clear. The sheer sides were coloured in a
weird blend of blues, greens, and whites. It was possible to
distinguish the different winters by the horizontal layers
of deeper-hued ice.

For the rest of that season we always kept a buoyboat
in close vicinity—just in case. The season was exciting in
other ways. It was the first year of World War II, and only
four pelagic expeditions ventured south—two British and
two Norwegian. Midway through the season a German
surface raider came on the scene and boarded and seized
both Norwegian factory vessels, thus gaining a season's
supply of whale-oil.

Now we were daily awaiting the signal to cease whaling
At last it came. Operations were to end at midnight on the
stated day. The leading whale-gunners now made frantic
attempts to keep their leading positions or overhaul one
another as to the number of whales killed. This was
specially important to the Norwegians, for great prestige

attaches to the leading whale-shooter of an expedition. He can pick his job, often on his own terms, and may get a very substantial retainer during the close season.

Whales still came, even in the worst of weather. We had reached our quota and could stop work now. But we still went on as hard as ever. We had passed our individual quota of whale-oil and were now on a 50-per-cent. increase on the bonus rate. But the days seemed long, and the nights longer, until the final day of the season at last came.

And there was the last whale of the season—a small fin, being hauled up the slipway.

The catcher vessels came alongside and refuelled for the last time, loading sufficient oil, water, and stores to enable them to reach South Georgia. A large part of their whaling equipment was dumped aboard the factory ship, and off they raced to base. Only the buoyboats remained to accompany us the nine hundred odd miles north-eastward to our island base. We were on our way home, engines at full speed.

Whaling watches were now suspended, and the entire ship's company (except for the watchkeepers) came on day-work. Sullen faces gave way to smiles; weariness was replaced by cheerfulness. We were more human, both physically and psychologically. Even the sea seemed more friendly, and the distant feathering of an occasional passing whale rated only a cursory glance. Time enough to get him next season!

Nobody could sleep the first night that we were free from operational whaling. It was much too quiet without the repeated clangs of the whale-claw and the roars of escaping steam as the steam pressure boilers were blown to the atmosphere. The night watchman made his rounds of a now silent ship.

The annual purification was started on board the factory ship—the job of making the ship look like a ship, of eradicating the grease, the blood, the guts, the grime, from the gigantic *abattoir*. Approximately twelve tons of caustic soda, along with other cleaning solvents, were used. Over two hundred whalemen began cleaning and disposal operations. Armed with axes and the heaviest of crowbars, a squad of flensers and labourers went about the job of tearing up the now badly worn whaling deck. The 30,000 square feet of timber deck-sheathing, which had been so meticulously laid on the outward voyage, was torn to pieces and thrown overboard. Our permanent wooden decks appeared—dirty and scarred, to be sure, but they would be dealt with later. Our wake for hundreds of miles astern was dotted with jetsam. Gear was dismantled, thoroughly cleaned, and stowed away until the next whaling season.

Solidified whale-oil, grease, blood, and grime were scraped from decks and superstructure. Everything and everywhere was scrubbed with caustic soda and near-boiling water.

We were preparing for arrival in South Georgia, where we would lay up the whale-catcher fleet. Nearly two hundred men would be discharged to spend the winter on the island. Equipment and surplus stores had to be landed, and we should load sufficient whale-oil to complete a full dead-weight cargo.

We wallowed behind our buoyboats, two tiny dots in a grey ocean. Icebergs were fewer, temperatures were rising —it was even time to start shedding clothes. Only the factory personnel, who had been labouring for the past twelve weeks in a temperature of 100° or more, felt the cold now. From the half-nude figures of a couple of days ago, they now went about their work muffled to the eyes in an assortment of hard-weather clothing.

Again South Georgia. There were the snow-clad peaks rising above the rolls of cumulus. The Gateway to the

Antarctic! If Antarctica can ever be forced to give up its presumed wealth, then the island of South Georgia may well become one of the most important points in the whole of the Western Hemisphere. It has the harbours, and it stands in the most strategic of positions relative to the Weddell Sea—the only area in the West where harbours, artificial or otherwise, could ever be constructed. Time will tell.

We made our way slowly into the bay and headed up for the tiny cleft which sheltered our land-based whaling station. A motor-boat roared away with our headlines to the shore. We had returned after a successful whaling season.

18

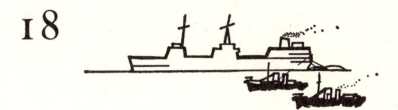

A month in jug in South Georgia

WHEN we got back to our island base there were the same scenes of bewildering activity as when we arrived. As soon as the first lines were fast to the shore our whole catcher fleet were jockeying for position to make fast alongside and get started on the job of laying up. All that remained to be done by the whaleboat crews was to get rid of their stores and moor their vessel for the winter. Factory-ship gangs went to work.

First the whale-lines were hove back on board and coiled in a heap that eventually reached mountainous proportions. They had done their duty in the Antarctic and were always renewed each season. There was always a ready market for old whale-lines. Stocks of harpoons, harpoon grenades, gunpowder, and the many other items of equipment were slung to the decks of the factory vessel. Compasses, sextants, chronometers, binoculars, and all the other paraphernalia of navigation had to be carefully stored. All that remained on board the catcher ships eventually were the harpoon guns. These were religiously tended by the whale-gunners and mates. After several coatings of grease had been applied the guns and their mounting were liberally covered with oily hessian. Then their exterior covers of canvas and oilskin were fitted. Accumulator blocks and springs had already been dismantled, oil and fresh water pumped out. The little ships were ready for the long winter's lay-up.

As each vessel was completed it was taken to its berth and securely moored by chain cables to embedded ground anchors and buoys. The whale-gunner and his crew packed their belongings and reported on board the factory vessel, to sign on for the long passage home. Their job was done.

On the other side of the whaling deck several gangs were discharging surplus stores and equipment for storage ashore. This would be picked up on the vessel's return for the next season. The bosun led a large gang on the shore side in this exacting and laborious work. Storage was some distance from the wharf, and, except for a somewhat ancient system of bogie transport, all equipment had to be manhandled. What the men lacked in the way of transport was made up with enthusiasm and energy. 'The quicker it's done the sooner we'll be homeward-bound' seemed to be the universal thought. Whale-oil and fuel-oil hoses were connected up between shore and factory ship. All surplus fuel was now pumped ashore, and we retained only enough to see us to our refuelling port on the voyage home—St Vincent, Cape Verde Islands. Whale-oil was loaded from shore storage to complete our full dead-weight cargo. This was our own oil. It had been ferried by tanker vessel during the season.

Cleaning operations continued. Gangs were constantly at this work. Caustic sprays, steam jets, and boiling water cascaded over the decks. The grease, the blood, and the guts—even the remaining paint—were torn away under this drastic treatment. The ship looked as if she had been sand-blasted. The steel plating slowly returned to its pre-whaling state. The same procedure went on below decks. All machinery was scraped before going through this caustic-and-hot-water treatment. The whale-boilers were cooked out for the last time, with clean, fresh water instead of whale. Slowly our great hulking factory ship returned to normal and began to smell clean and fresh.

The island's magistrate and his limited staff, along with our own secretaries, were busy at this stage. Even South Georgia's one and only policeman had to lend a hand. There was a mass of paper-work in the signing off and on of crews. Hundreds of men flitted about from ship to shore and shore to ship, transferring baggage and searching for accommodation. The ship was a proper bedlam.

Amazingly, even to the executives who controlled it all, everything seemed to smooth itself out, and all personnel was settled and even happy. Vacant storerooms, surgery waiting-rooms, and various offices were used to accommodate the overflow of men. Who cared where he slept? Soon we would be under way.

I got talking to the island's representative of law and order—the Criminal Investigation Department, Riot Squad, and Constabulary all rolled into one.

"Have you had much trouble with law-breakers during your long stay her?" I inquired innocently.

He looked down with withering scorn, wondering if I was serious. "No," he replied. "The only trouble I ever have is when some of these ruddy over-winterers start experimenting with an illicit still. Then there's plenty trouble. There are usually some smart lads among the over-winterers—especially you Scots."

"What happens then?"

He smiled grimly. "They find themselves landed in the jug for a month or two. The magistrate won't stand for it—not nowadays."

I pumped one of the older Shetlanders, who I knew had spent many winters on the island, about South Georgia's prison.

"A month in jug?" he exclaimed. "Aye . . . it's happened. The magistrate is strict about such monkey-business. It suits him to get a couple of whalemen in jug for a month or two. He gets all the painting done around the Government post for damn all. And it's a funny gaol that has no key; and a queer set-up when the prisoner has to call the gaoler with an early-morning cup of tea. I know—I've been there."

There was little to do in the factory ship during these South Georgia evenings. A film programme was shown every night, but few went to see it. Many preferred meeting, and swapping yarns with, their island friends. Others found greater enjoyment in getting down to a good book.

"You know what surprised me most about your ruddy whalemen?" a boffin said to me. "When once you break down their granite reserve and get them into a conversational mood, they can usually talk at length on any subject, with intelligence and information. It doesn't matter what the subject is. They usually know much more about it than a mere landlubber like myself. It really is strange. One would imagine they would be out of touch with most things going on in the world. But they're not."

He didn't know that the chief enjoyment of present-day whalemen, as well as of the deep-water seamen, is reading. A book a day is not an uncommon appetite—and it's not all fiction. This reading, along with the news from radio bulletins, seems to give them a knowledge of current affairs well above that of the average shore-dweller, who usually finds time only for the latest football or Test score and a bit of scandal from the national newspapers.

Thanks to that excellent body the Seafarers' Education Services, sailors are now given every opportunity for study and advancement. It is possible to sit for various examinations while actually at sea. It has been done frequently.

Whale-gunners usually got together within our circle in the evenings to talk over their experiences. Many had tales of woeful luck, of bad whaleboats, and of inefficient crews. These were the unsuccessful. The successful ones listened to these hard-luck stories with an air of superior detachment, as if there were no such thing as bad luck, bad catcher vessels, or bad crews. Glasses of aquavit, the Norwegian national drink, littered the tables, and, as the evening progressed, so the whales these heroes had so recently tackled and killed became more and more formidable and gigantic, so that it seemed a miracle we ever got them up the whale-slipway. Whalemen say that aquavit should be aged in the cask and properly mellowed by a sea voyage with a double crossing of the equator. Unfortunately, it usually made only a one-way journey.

Another job we enjoyed during these days was a fishing expedition. This augmented our homeward fresh-food supplies, and the catch was gratefully received by the chief steward. Our food supplies were usually low at this stage. Some of our storerooms were even used to accommodate the whale-catcher crews. When I looked at the result of a few hour's fishing—gutted, cleaned, and nicely arranged on deck—I always realized how very little of the world's sea areas were exploited. What potentiality there must be in the far-distant reaches for trawlers accompanied by a parent vessel. An inexhaustible amount—ready for the taking. So far we have only dabbled at the fringes.

Our efficient storekeeper was now one of the most important and active men aboard. He had a hundred and one duties that required his own supervision. He usually had a couple of helpers, but nobody liked the job. The storekeeper was very hard to please. He kept his storerooms immaculate; his books were neater and more precise than any book-keeper's, and, what was more important, he could put his hands on anything that was wanted.

I listened to him one day from the doorway of his store. He was giving one of his helpers hell. "Come on," he was shouting, "put that damned cigarette out! You can't work and smoke at the same time." His lackadaisical assistant, splicing away at some sort of rope tackle, looked up with a hurt and innocent expression. "Who the hell's working?" he inquired. The storekeeper gave a sort of gulp and was speechless.

Each season, before the factory ship sailed for home, a few whalemen paid a visit to the small cemetery on the outskirts of the whaling station. Here, close by a small glacial stream which everlastingly flowed to the open sea, were the graves of men who had lost their lives while doing their duty—men who had died with their boots on. The graves were all carefully tended and topped by a small headstone giving the name and age of the whaleman and the year of his passing. Whalemen are at heart a simple people. Their job makes them so. Beneath their rough exteriors they are generous and spontaneous. During the many expeditions in which I have taken part I have never known an occasion when the death of a fellow-whaleman failed to produce a generous subscription for his dependents. Perhaps it wasn't a great thing to do. It didn't amount to much from each man—maybe a pound or two. Still, there were over six hundred men with each expedition.

I like to think it helped those at home who had lost a breadwinner. . . .

The men who stay behind

WHAT of these over-winterers? These men who volunteered to remain in South Georgia during the Antarctic winter for maintenance and overhaul to catcher fleets?

Upward of four hundred men were employed each winter at this island. Work was supposed to be an eight-hour day, but overtime was necessary at all times, and Saturday afternoon was the only time for a few leisure-hours of recreation. They say man can get used to any environment. You were convinced this was true when you saw the monotony, the dreariness, and the drabness of working in such surroundings. True, wages were good, and there was the overtime; but money was poor compensation for eighteen months away from home in such conditions. Two whaling seasons and one over-wintering period all add up to a healthy-looking pay-off cheque at the end. But the men earned every penny of it.

Take the housing, to start with. It consisted of squalid and unhealthy-looking barrack-like structures made of timber and corrugated iron. Each barracks housed about fifty men in four-berth cabins. The smells in them were unbelievably foul—smells accumulated from successive generations of whalemen. The system of sanitation was prehistoric. A shore-based whaling station is probably about the filthiest habitation of men the whole world over.

Then the sun was never seen for months. As it slowly reached its maximum daily altitude it was always obscured by the towering and rugged peaks that overlooked the station. It was a great day for these over-winterers when the sun again reached a sufficiently southerly declination to show over the mountain-tops. This meant the spring had arrived. Soon the factory ship would be heading south. The Antarctic winter was nearly over.

South Georgia winds are probably the fiercest and wildest in the world—not excepting a West Indian hurricane. Squalls almost constantly roar down from the glaciers, bringing icy blasts that often reach a force of 150 miles an hour. It was no wonder that all houses had to be anchored to the ground to prevent them being hurled into the sea. During such winds it was safest to stay put, for the corrugated iron from the roofs of buildings was liable to become detached and to fly through the air as if it were sheets of paper.

During the winter the island was a scene of wild and rugged beauty. Snow covered the ground, sometimes to a depth of ten to twelve feet in drifts. Avalanches from the neighbouring peaks crashed into the waters at intervals, tumbling with a muffled roar as they gathered momentum down the slopes of the mountains. The whaling station was located well clear of these frightening hazards— hazards that sometimes end in tragedy for any wandering whaleman.

The catcher fleets lay moored line abreast like a swarm of derelict fighting ships, their low hulls and superstructures covered in a shroud of virgin snow. "What a bastard of a place!" remarked one of the tradesmen who was spending his first winter on South Georgia. "What do they call it? 'Gateway to Antarctica?' 'Gateway to Hell' would be more appropriate!' He looked round the frozen landscape with disgust, and continued, "Look at the living-quarters, the sanitary arrangements. Hell! It was like this fifty years ago, the same now as when the bloody place was built. To get to the latrines you've got to walk through two or three feet of snow, stepping over ruddy sea-elephants as you go. No, sir, no more South Georgia for me."

Many whalemen talked like this; but each year they headed again for the South to a job they detested, but found irresistible. They would have been unhappy in any other work. The daily labours began at 8 A.M. and continued except for a couple of meal-hours, until 9 P.M., when all work ceased for the day. A solitary watchman took over then, patrolling the silent buildings and workshops in case of fire, while the whole station slept. Watching these whalemen line up to begin a day's work always fascinated me. They were tough, bearded, weatherbeaten men, waiting to receive their orders from the foreman. They were Norwegians and Scots mainly, with a minority of Englishmen.

Close friendships were formed among the national groups, of course, but they were never clannish. The whaler from Tönsberg was just as sociable with the man from Tyneside as he was with one of his fellow-townsmen, and vice versa. The main thing was the job in hand, and this was always done with great efficiency and speed by all members of a working-gang. There were no language difficulties. Most Norwegians spoke fluent English, and

many of the British whalemen spoke passable Norsk—
especially when it came to swearing.

Within minutes of receiving their daily orders the fore-
men had their gangs at work. During the winter about
forty catcher ships had to be dry-docked, repaired, serviced,
and repainted. This work alone involved considerable
organization. Weather was not at all suitable for constant
work in a floating dry-dock. Chances had to be taken—
and were taken cheerfully—so that the close season's
commitments could be carried out. No sooner was one
vessel undocked than another took its place. Work went
on with clockwork precision. Teams of whaleboat men,
headed by engineers, mates, and tradesmen, were responsible for all repairs and maintenance to the catcher fleet.
Each gang came under the direction of the station engineer.
He had the authority to survey and pass each vessel, both
for seaworthiness and insurance purposes.

In and around the whaling station outdoor gangs went
about their labours heavily clad against the biting southerly
winds and freezing temperatures. The mornings were the
worst. Sometimes men spent two hours clearing snow
before they could get to the job of the night before.
Occasionally a really heavy fall reached a depth of six feet
during the night. The whole station was alerted to deal
with this tiresome hazard. It meant danger to the catcher
fleet. This was dangerous and hard work.

We had such a snowfall the winter I stayed on the island.
Within a few hours it was four feet deep—considerably
more in the drifts. Two score of catcher vessels lay at their
moorings in a state of chaos. They were like ghostly and
derelict ships as they heeled over at alarming angles
because of the weight of snow that covered them. A major
catastrophe seemed imminent. Very quickly two hundred
or more whalemen boarded the vessels to clear the snow.
Slowly the whaleboats righted themselves and began to

look more secure to our anxious eyes. A neighbouring station wasn't so fortunate. One of their vessels capsized.

It was a difficult task to keep the main paths through the station free from snow and ice. There were no modern machines for the job. Everything had to be done by hand, except for the use of steam exhausts. Hoses led steam to the strategic points and kept them clear. But let the ignorant or the unwary whaleman deviate from the known paths, and he would land in trouble—plenty trouble. It was dangerous to go far from the station in winter. There were frequent avalanches, and wanderers were liable to get lost in the undulating ridges. Or they might get bogged down in mushy snowdrifts. It was safer to stay at home.

There were usually casualties on Saturday, and the station's medical officer was kept busy. This was when the young and the not-so-young whalemen tried to organize a bit of sport by turning the near-by area into a winter resort. Out came skis and toboggans. Even sheets of corrugated steel were used, to get up a crazy speed down the snow-clad slopes. The Norwegians were naturally very efficient at all winter sports. But some of the British whalemen had learnt the hard way by simple trial and error.

Scattered round in the snow and ice, and always exposed to the climate, lay thousands of pounds' worth of what had once been new equipment. It was equipment which never seemed to be required or utilized. It had perhaps been requisitioned for one occasion and then duplicated year after year. Mixed up with all this new stuff were condemned machine parts, dilapidated electric motors, old pressure boilers, boiler tubes, and various catcher machinery—a vast junk-yard. Nobody seemed to worry, least of all the office staff who stayed at home.

My trips round the coast of South Georgia during winter months led me to several harbours where whaling and sealing had been done in the not-so-distant past. These

stations still stood, desolated and silent. Their buildings
and machinery crumbled into decay and ruin as the huge
business interests, whose property they were, abandoned
them utterly to the elements so that they could reach out
grasping hands southward in search of whale—and dividends. One such station held an irresistible fascination for
me—perhaps because of its surroundings. The harbour
had been well chosen. It was a natural inlet, completely
sheltered from the sea and surrounded on three sides by
a rugged mountain range, which rose at most places sheer
from the water to sharp peaks. Along the narrow foreshore, broken by rocks of fantastic shapes, huge masses of
seaweed grew up from the bottom and reached out their
ribbon-like fronds to act as a natural breakwater. The
seaweed covered the whole harbour. I have heard it said
that common seaweed has about fifty different uses; that
it has become so valuable that new industries have been
created to deal with its properties. If this is so, then here
must be money. Round the coast of South Georgia and
other Southern Ocean islands the supply of this kelp seems
inexhaustible.

We often sent the service boat, skippered by the same
old worthy I have already described, and manned by a
crowd of over-winterers, to this abandoned whaling station.
We were usually on the scrounge for materials. Timber,
steel girders, even old whale-boilers came in useful to
maintain our station. Every one was eager to go on such an
expedition. There was good fishing, maybe a chance of
killing a sea-leopard. Above all, it was a change from the
daily grind of a winter's routine. The party consisted of
fourteen men—all that the service boat could take. It was
with a sense of adventure that we set off, although the
station was only about fifty miles away. But the short sea-
passage often proved a great trial to some of our tradesmen.
They were not used to little ships. Whaleboat life, even at

its best, is uncomfortable. For a part-time seaman it can be hell. It demands three things—a strong stomach, a stout heart, and a willingness to live dangerously. Our poor tradesmen lacked the strong stomach.

You can't cure a seasick man. You can't help him. You can't even terrify him. He is, to all intents and purpose—dead. It was with great amusement that some of us watched the misfortunes of others.

As we steamed close inshore we could see the ruggedness and utter loneliness of the island. The interior must be still more awesome. Among the huge mountains of sterile rock were numerous glaciers, whose green-and-blue translucent ice-tops gleamed brightly even in the sickly light of winter. We entered the harbour and moored at a dilapidated wharf. Everywhere there was a desolation of untrodden snow. A score or more of ramshackle buildings, their wooden sides bulging or gaping wide open, were clustered in the main part of the station.

Above what had once been the boiler-houses two steel chimneys rose high and swung crazily in the wind. Another lay where it had crashed through the roof of the blacksmith's shop, where forges, anvils, and other tools still stood just as they had been left thirty years before. Across the harbour a storage shed of huge capacity was partly demolished. Wrecking gangs, such as we were, had been here before. A sunken, dismasted barque, its bows covered with seaweed, rose out of the leaden depths like some prehistoric monster.

A crowd of sea-elephants littered the narrow patch of foreshore like gigantic brown slugs. A solitary penguin, lonely and pathetic, waited for its mate. Here was a loneliness that touched the imagination. There was no to-day, no to-morrow, only the for ever. It gave one the sense that something had passed by—something of significance. It remined us, too, that we were passing, and with us this so-called modern era. It will be the same a hundred years from now. What is a century in the evolution of nature?

Our working-party were soon at work. On this trip we wanted to dismantle a huge water-tube boiler from the power-house and get it transported back to our own base. No matter how tough the job we always managed somehow to get it done. As an old factory ship's doctor once said to me when things were going badly, "The impossible we can do right away. Miracles take a little longer."

Our stay on each of these foraging trips lasted three or four days. Getting the stuff we wanted to the service boat was the worst part of the work. Everything had to be manhandled. We made sledges for transporting, and the ship's lifeboats often came in useful for ferrying gear from one part of the station to another. We weren't concerned so much with the niceties of the job. Our greatest concern was just how quickly it could be done. Take whale-boilers, for example. Each weighed about three tons and was mounted on a solid-brickwork foundation about four feet high. We had no time to dismantle the foundations. That would have taken many days. But a couple of holes chiselled or drilled into the brickwork, then a couple of small charges of dynamite and presto! the whole works collapsed —our whale-boiler as well. The water-tube boiler referred to was a different proposition. We got it down all right, much to our satisfaction. But twelve tons of bulky material is a difficult job to move, especially by hand. The boiler rested among a debris of broken bricks and mortar inside a more-than-dilapidated building. The nearest foreshore was more than three hundred yards away. We all gazed at it, wondering if it would beat us.

Then one of the Shetlanders shouted, "Put the ruddy whaleboat on to it." The simplicity of his reasoning was its strength. That's exactly what we did. I got the whaleboat backed as close to the foreshore as possible. A four-inch wire was connected between it and the water-tube boiler, and, after several attempts, the huge object came hurtling through the boiler-house and within minutes was on the beach. What the hell did it matter if we had taken the building as well? The boiler was rapidly and efficiently plugged and the whole contraption towed to our own station fifty miles away—a day's work.

A few years ago I visited the port of Bluff, in New Zealand. This small oyster-fishing town is the seaport for the industrial city of Invercargill—the most densely populated region in the Southland of New Zealand. In one of the many tourist brochures which I scrutinized I noticed this statement: "Dog Island light, at the entrance to the port of Bluff, is the most southerly light in the Southern Hemisphere."

Actually, this is not quite correct, for there are two navigational lights on the island of South Georgia that are shown on the charts. Both are entered in the Admiralty List of Lights. There used to be three, the third being at the entrance of this old whaling harbour. I should know: I took it down.

We had been spending a few days at this harbour on various duties. Among them was the job of dismantling two high and bulky aerial masts. I decided to dismantle the derelict light as well. We got it down, complete with its fittings, and transported the lot back to the small, sandy strip of beach where we had left the whaleboat's lifeboat. As it was comparatively early we decided to scout along the foreshore, in the hope of seeing a sea-leopard. We didn't find one. As we returned to the lifeboat to ferry our stuff back to the catcher vessel, which we had left five miles away, a sudden and unexpected squall arose. Instead of passing over quickly, as usually was the case, the wind continued. The skies became leaden, and the surface of the harbour soon whipped up into a whirling maelstrom. To attempt the short passage back to the whaleboat would have been foolhardy. We sought what shelter we could among the rocks. The afternoon passed, and the skies became blacker as the wind increased. Snow and driving sleet set in, and the outlook was grim. I flooded the lifeboat to avoid its being broken up by the continuous pounding of the waves. We decided to make the journey back to the catcher vessel on foot.

Five miles isn't far, but over such terrain it can be a hell of a job. We crawled along the narrow foreshore, constantly climbing over rocks. We bypassed a dangerous glacier by going around the face of it—a nerve-shattering experience. The light of a Southern winter's afternoon was fading. Many of the rocks were littered with enormous bull sea-elephants. By a simple swish of their tails they could have sent any of us to kingdom-come. We got back to the whaleboat at last, but we were a bunch of miserable and dejected figures. There was one consolation—we didn't have to spend the night in the open. Next morning we retrieved our lifeboat, still undamaged, and along with it our Southern Ocean navigational light.

Fish were abundant at this harbour. A meal for fourteen men could be caught in about twenty minutes. I often slipped off to catch the evening's meal as the whalemen worked. I was once fishing here with a hand-line from a small boat. Business was rather slack, and I wasn't much interested in my immediate surroundings. To stop my small boat drifting I had tied up to a large mass of kelp that grew up from the sea-bottom. Suddenly a mighty shape shot up vertically, right alongside the small boat. It was a sea-leopard! I seized an oar and was about to bring it down on the animal's head when I thought it might be safer not to be a man of wrath. Instead, I quickly cut the boat adrift and quietly skulled the small craft back to the catcher vessel. The sea-leopard followed. Its long neck supported a ferocious and evil-looking face. Its mouth, with bared fangs, was almost in my boat all the way back. It seemed a long time until I got to the whaleboat. At last I was alongside and jumped safely aboard. I grabbed a rifle and went to the side. But the sea-leopard had vanished.

I discussed this adventure with a group of old-timers— men who had spent many winters on South Georgia. They all agreed that if I had hit the animal it would certainly have attacked. Probably its first action would have been to capsize the boat. Then I should have been at its mercy. The best sea-leopards are dead ones. One day I shot one as it lay basking on the rocks. It slept—and never woke up. Several of the Shetland seamen helped me to get the cadaver back to the service boat. I watched them go about the business of flensing and saving the valuable skin. It was first slit down the belly, and the skin, with part of the blubber still attached, was delicately removed from the carcass with razor-sharp knives. In the meantime a large wooden stretching-frame, roughly eighteen by twelve feet, had been constructed. The skin was tautly stretched on it. Then the remaining blubber was carefully scraped away, and the skin was ready for the curing process. At frequent intervals during the next four weeks the skin was liberally treated with alum. It was kept taut on its frame, and at last the trophy emerged. It was a rich and splendid prize for any hunter.

There was nothing to do in the evenings during our stays at this harbour. We carried no working-lights, and darkness set in by 4 P.M. To compensate for this early knocking-off-time we worked throughout the meal-times. We had the radio, and we carried plenty of books and magazines, but these luxuries can be galling at times. We could sleep, of course, or we might muster up enough courage to poke a nose out into the freezing atmosphere and observe the heavens of the Southern Hemisphere.

During still nights infinite multitudes of stars shone

down on the eerie and ghostly harbour. The Southern Cross constellation, so well known to navigators, rode high in the sky. Its four great stars were imposing, but equally impressive were the two Centauris which rode in neighbourly proximity. The planets made their journey across the heavens like young moons, leaving a golden wake behind them—a soft, glowing beauty.

Now and then the Aurora Australis would put on a show. These brilliant curtains of coloured lights spread across the sky, faded, and then reappeared more intensely. The Southern Lights are similar to the Aurora Borealis of the North. Both are caused by streams of electrical particles ejected from the sun and attracted by the earth's Magnetic Poles.

When we were at this harbour we often got the service boat's old skipper talking of his young days. Then all the flensing and cutting-up of whales had to be done from overside.

"We had to steam far into the pack-ice to get the necessary shelter for the job. And a bloody wet and cold job it was. It was cold enough to freeze a brass monkey.

"We used to lie within the shelter of Deception Island for months on end. Our catchers would go out and scour the neighbouring waters. They brought the cadavers back for processing. It wasn't so bad there. We lay to our anchors with the stern moored to the shore. Working up the whales was no trouble at all, but we had to get the hell out of it as soon as it started to freeze.

"Then there were the South Orkney Islands. We used to go round them like a bloody merry-go-round, looking for a lee and shelter. Twelve weeks of whaling? Hell, in those days we did six months, and if there were no whales to work we were down in the holds trimming coal. There was no oil fuel then and no air-conditioning throughout the ship. It was cold—damned cold."

Every one has heard the story of the Three Bears. The old skipper had a version of his own, which he quoted with great seriousness to anyone who got disgruntled with his unhappy lot. His three bears were polar bears. They had wandered far from their home in the Arctic to the Antarctic and landed on Deception Island. They looked around them to take their bearings—the great father bear, the mother bear, and the tiny baby bear. The father bear shivered as he surveyed the bleakness of Deception—the grey iciness of the place and the frozen waters. "Hell!" he exclaimed. "When I get back home I'll have a tale to be told."

The mother bear nodded in agreement. "And me," she said. "What a place! When I get home I too have a tale to be told."

The baby bear, snuggling close to his parents on the rocky foreshore, pricked his ears and said, "Come on, let's *go* home. My tail *is* cold."

The old skipper elaborated on the story—especially to whalemen who growled at the vile conditions. "There's a moral in that little story," he said. Eventually somebody was compelled to ask what was the moral.

"Well, always find out where and what you are going to before leaving home," said the old skipper.

One of our most frequent over-winterers was a canine—a brown-haired husky named Lassie. She was adopted as a pup by one of the whale-gunners, who had her from a meteorological expedition. Lassie was a magnificent animal. Her coat was shaggy and of a deep rusty colour. Broad in the chest, she always carried her head high with her ears erect. As all husky dogs seem to be, she looked the epitome of strength. And she was a one-man dog.

She knew nothing except the life of whaling ships and the men who manned them. Her whole life had been spent on such vessels. She loved and obeyed her master to an extraordinary degree and sailed with him every season. When the whaleboats were laid up for the winter poor Lassie grieved for her master, who sailed away on the factory vessel. She didn't seem to want company. She was always alone and silent. She was carefully fed by the station cooks, but always lived on the now silent catcher ship that had been her home during the previous season. The winter must have passed slowly for Lassie. She only came ashore for food, then returned to the whaleboat to wait for her master's return. She seemed to know when the new season was approaching. She became lively and would now romp round the station, to every one's amazement. When at last the whale-gunner did arrive back, there was Lassie waiting for him on the wharf, just as she had waited all winter. And the welcome he got touched every one's heart.

Lassie was in her element during whale-hunting. She cared nothing for the weather. She just shook off the icy sprays that constantly poured over the catcher's decks. When there was a chase on she rose to a pitch of intense excitement. She dashed from the bridge to the harpoon gun, looking up into her master's face as if imploring him to shoot. As the gunner took up his stand by the gun Lassie was at his feet, and every time the whale surfaced the dog bared her teeth and howled as only a husky can. Then, as the whale sounded again, she seemed to sense the direction in which the track would lead. She faced this direction and nearly went frantic, as if she was ready to dive overboard and follow. The whale-gunner always altered his course to the point which Lassie indicated, sometimes against his own judgment. And she was usually right. Now, how did she know which way the whale had gone?

Lassie's only prize when at last the whale was killed was a small piece of gristle cut from the tail. She stood over this for hours and defied everyone, even her master, to take it from her. That is, until the next whale was sighted.

And so our spell at the island of South Georgia came to an end. We had topped up to a full dead-weight cargo. Whale-oil worth £1,500,000 filled our cargo tanks, and we had all of the by-products. Our catcher fleet were safely laid up for their yearly overhaul and maintenance. We had signed off our over-wintering personnel and had embarked our catcher crews and others who were going home. Everything at last was ready for us to return to civilization, to warmth, to comfort, to the reward of all our labours, to those who waited for us at home.

The over-winterers watched us go. We felt a pang of pity for them as they waved us away. For us there was the joy of looking forward.

20

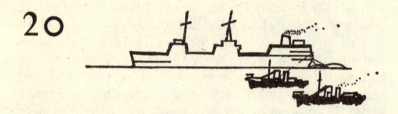

Home is the sailor

WE bade farewell to the bleak, sterile, sullen-looking island. As we slowly manœuvred astern on the twin engines, swung round in the bay, and headed for the entrance we were watched by the four hundred over-winterers for whom there would no be happy home-coming this year. A last series of blasts of farewell on the siren, which were echoed back to us from the mountains, and we passed out of sight. The course was set for the northward, and we were really homeward-bound.

What had the season brought us? What had it brought the six-hundred-odd whalemen who comprised the expedition's personnel? What had it brought in kind? And what had it brought the whaling firm whose interests we served?

We were one of the successful expeditions. We had pro-cessed nearly twenty-five thousand tons of whale-oil from approximately two thousand seven hundred whales killed and worked up. We had well over three thousand tons of meat- and liver-meal compactly stowed in our cargo tanks. And we had our quota of liver-oil and other by-products. It doesn't look much on paper. Yet the twelve-week operations had netted a total of nearly £3 million—a lot of money. It had brought the nation a large percentage of its oils and fats. It had provided work for thousands of people only remotely connected with the whale, and it had provided a living for the whalemen—at the expense of the whale.

It has been suggested, even by the whalemen themselves —especially when they have had a few drinks—that the emoluments earned on a pelagic whaling expedition are fantastic. This is stuff and nonesense! The wages and bonus expectations seem good—but only on paper. Look what it entails. The job is only a seasonal one—seven months out of the twelve. Only 5 per cent. of the personnel are employed throughout the year. On the whaling grounds work is scheduled for ten hours a day, but lasts twelve— day- and night-gangs each working a round of the clock seven days a week. There is no let-up, and work goes on whatever the conditions. There may blow a howling, freezing gale—the cutting-up and processing of whales still has to go on. There are no Saturday afternoons and Sundays off. Work is carried out in freezing temperatures on deck and in boiling, humid conditions below deck.

The whaleman comes home. He has a nice pay-off—so much per month, a bonus on the result of the expedition's production, and his overtime. Omit the overtime and what have you left? A mere labourer's wage, paid for work done in conditions that defy description, work done with frenzied abandon and a willingness unknown in any other walk of life; seven months and his bonus. It seems a lot of money, but only because he has spent nothing during those exacting months. Once ashore the accumulated wages soon go, and within a month or two he is looking round for another job, any job, until such time as another whaling expedition goes south for another season.

Whale-gunners are said to receive princely salaries. Their wages are good and for a few—very few—might be called 'princely.' Only 20 per cent. of the whale-shooters earn big money. The rest lag far behind. They are paid by the actual number and length of the whales killed, and it is simple logic that if they don't get these numbers they lose out on the deal. The greatest losers, of course, would be the whaling firms.

As for the whaling crews—there is no overtime here. They work a twenty-four-hour day from start to finish of the season. Sleep is taken mainly in cat-naps, and they have to be ready for a call at any time of the day or night. A monthly wage and a share—a very small fractional share—in the kill of their own ship, that is their season's wages. The crews of the buoyboats and towing vessels receive an average award of the combined operational fleet. Often they are better off.

We soon shifted our latitude now. Three hundred miles a day, steaming due north, decreases the parallels by 5° daily. The temperature began to rise. This was tropical weather to us, compared with what we had experienced during the last four months. The icebergs were gone. There are few barrier icebergs north of South Georgia. Although ice can be met with up to five hundred miles north of the island, the bergs are mostly pinnacle-shaped, similar to the glacial icebergs of the Northern Hemisphere. This is due to constant calving, as the original iceberg grows smaller as it drifts north. Erosion and melting occur, and what was once part of the great ice barrier of Antarctica becomes part of the waters of the South Atlantic Ocean.

The navigation personnel could relax now. No need to be for ever on the alert for the sudden appearance, out of the blackness, of the greyish blur that meant an iceberg at hand. Now there were only the leaden waters of the South Atlantic and our friends the albatrosses. They circled round us with their gliding sweeps, wondering where the food had gone. Why had the fatty titbits ceased? All through the forties they followed us—then suddenly they were gone.

The sun, which somehow always looked weak and sickly in the higher latitudes, now came to life. It was actually warm. Beards were shaved off as the men discarded their heavier clothing. Many of these clean-shaven types could hardly be recognized as the bearded, harassed workmen of a couple of weeks back.

Gangs were at work everywhere. The smell of whale, an integral part of a whaleship, had been eradicated, or so it seemed to us, and we began to paint ship. Teams of men, about twenty to a squad, headed by a foreman or a whale-catcher mate, were each allotted a portion of deck or factory. Rust was removed, several coatings of anti-corrosive were applied, and the section was completed by applications of the best enamels. Work tempo was much slower than on the outward voyage. We had plenty of time. Our whaleship, our hulking whale-oil refinery, would soon look as smart as any ocean-going liner; as trim and efficient as any man-of-war—except for the speed.

We chugged along at a little better than twelve knots, but every hour was bringing us twelve miles nearer home. We had spent the summer in the South. Now we were going to spend the summer in the North. We followed the sun. Hell, we were good-weather sailors!

In the factory spaces tradesmen went about their daily toils. There was the machinery to clean and overhaul.

The whale-boilers and their various attachments had to be dealt with, separating-machinery and electric motors had to be serviced. We were already preparing for next season.

Meal-times were hectic for the catering staff. It was no easy job to accommodate nearly six hundred men at one sitting in a limited space. And no one complained if some of the personnel edged towards the mess-rooms a little before time.

We sailed through the 'roaring forties', where gales are frequent, especially in winter; where the weather is usually overcast and subject to rapid changes, where fine weather seldom lasts long and the prevailing winds are from the westward; the latitudes where the windjammers of old set up records as they raced their cargoes home.

Through the parallels of the thirties and the twenties and into the tropics. We enjoyed it all, every minute of it, after four months along the ice edge of Antarctica.

Isle de Trinidade lay to starboard, a pinprick in the chart of the South Atlantic, an inhabited island of volcanic origin rising out of the ocean to a height of nearly two thousand feet. The depth of water surrounding the tiny islet is about two thousand six hundred fathoms; so the peak rises from the ocean-bed to a height of nearly eighteen thousand feet.

One season, when we were accompanied home by four whale-catcher vessels, this island provided a lee for refuelling these whaleboats. The factory vessel was stopped close to the leeward of the island, and the catcher vessels were taken alongside in turn for refuelling.

The first whaleboat had received fuel enough to see it to the next refuelling point and had taken aboard stores and fresh water, and now lay off, waiting for the other three ships. The whale-gunner edged his vessel close to shore. He had been studying the South Atlantic Pilot and was full of information about Trinidade. "Come on," he said. "Let's lower a boat and see if we can kill a couple of these wild hogs that are supposed to abound here. Let's land and have a look-see." The crew eagerly obeyed. The lifeboat was lowered and manned by the gunner himself, the chief engineer, and four members of the crew, made its way towards the beach.

There was a moderate surf breaking, so the gunner decided that only himself and the engineer should be landed. The others were to lie off until such time as the boat was required again, to get the dead hogs on board and to embark the intrepid hunters. Clutching their rifles, the two men managed to scramble ashore, though not without a ducking. The rugged mass of rock and vegetation rose nearly sheer from the tiny beach. A waterfall, which seemed at one time to have cascaded a considerable torrent of water into the open sea, now ran a mere trickle. The hunters began tracking wild pigs. They made their way upward over rock and scrub, but there were no pigs. Indeed, the island seemed barren of life, so after an hour's search they decided to return. There would be no pork for supper, and the crew would be disappointed. But the catcher vessels would have finished refuelling, and it was time to get under way.

But when they looked at the downward track the whole area was seething with a mass of gigantic, slimy, loathsome land-crabs. They seemed to be coming from everywhere and converging on the spot where they stood.

"Let's get the hell out of this," shouted the chief. "The bastards are after us!" It had taken them an hour's hard, strenuous effort to make the outward journey. They returned in ten minutes flat. Every time I heard this anecdote the crabs grew larger and larger.

We enjoyed our spell in the tropics. As we approached the equator most of the men were bronzed and sun-

tanned. You would never have guessed they had just
come from Antarctica. We had rigged the swimming-pool
again, and it was used day and night. A new movie programme was shown on deck every second evening, as we
had exchanged films with one of the sister expeditions.
But time began to drag. We all felt the expectant excitement that is always with the home-coming seamen. The
whaling deck in the evenings presented a scene as busy as
an Aberdeen street on a day of a house-to-house collection.
Hundreds of whalemen walked the decks far into the night
hours. They couldn't sleep. They were suffering from the
neurosis that has been called 'the Channels' by many
generations of seamen, a neurosis that no home-coming
deep-water seaman can escape.

Across the equator and into the Northern Hemisphere.
There is no crossing-the-line and Father Neptune ritual
on whale-factory ships now—not since pre-war days. We
did have the ceremony one year as we were bound south,
but it ended in fiasco and has never been repeated.

It was done in style, and all personnel except the watchkeepers had been granted a half-day. The manager had
delegated his duties to the ship's secretary, and the steward
had been told to splice the main brace at the end of the
proceedings.

As the ship's bell tolled one of the deck officers greeted
Father Neptune and his staff as they clambered over the
stem. Freedom of the ship was given, and they went aft
where the King's throne had been erected by the swimming-
pool. There was a small band with a nucleus of two
accordionists. Neptune, a gigantic, brawny Shetland flenser, strode ahead, carrying a huge gold trident, followed
by Queen Aphrodite in her queenly regalia, with a huge
necklace of sperm-teeth round her neck. Then came the
harem, followed by the doctor and the barber carrying the
implements of their trade, except that the barber had a

flensing-knife for a razor. After them the Clerk of the Court, the policeman, and the various bears dressed in the most elaborate costumes.

The court opened. Each of the offenders (the first-trippers) was accused of loitering in the Northern Hemisphere and sentenced. They were tended by the doctor and the barber before being dumped in the pool to be roughly handled by the bears. As each culprit was pulled from the bath the Clerk of the Court issued him with the appropriate certificate, and the chief steward issued a large shot of rum and a bottle of beer to each of the initiated whalemen. The proceedings ended by splicing the main brace to all the ship's personnel. But the now somewhat dilapidated Aphrodite thought it too early to finish. "Let's get around and dump some of these ruddy executives and whale-gunners," she shouted. "Let's get hold of them—a drink or a ducking!"

No sooner said than done, and the Neptune squad scoured the officers' accommodation for victims. There was no ceremonial dress or ceremony now. They got a lot of rebuffs, a lot of victims, and a lot of drinks. I finally put an end to the festivities by removing the plug from the swimming-pool—then I worried throughout the dark hours lest some whaleman should dive into the now empty pool.

St Vincent, Cape Verde Islands, lay behind us. It is a barren-looking island composed of mountains of volcanic origin, the largest of a group of fourteen islands. It has no vegetation apart from a little tamarisk scrub, and water is scarce. Large amounts have to be imported from neighbouring islands. There is no cultivation. We stayed only long enough to load fuel to last out the voyage. Fresh eggs and vegetables, both of poor quality, were taken on board, and four hours after coming to anchorage we were under way again. We were now on the last stretch, bound for Tönsberg, to disembark our Norwegian personnel before proceeding to Liverpool to sign off the Britishers and discharge our cargo of whale-oil and by-products.

Slowly—too slowly for us—we increased the parallels of latitude. We sighted part of the Canary Islands group and passed the island of Madeira somewhere to the westward. The North Star, Polaris, lay just to the port side of our stem and grew higher in altitude every evening. We were steaming direct for Finisterre, the southerly point of the Bay of Biscay. We were nearly home.

The whaleship was looking at its best, with everything in immaculate order. The working-gangs were putting final touches to what had been a pleasant three weeks' work. There was little work done during the last three days of the homeward passage. The job had been carried out efficiently, and there was a semi-official Stand Easy. Now was the time to get one's gear packed, to prepare for leaving the ship.

The great, beamy whale-deck was quite barren of equipment. With a couple of goal-posts stuck up it would have looked like a miniature football-field. The permanent wooden deck was snow-white, as immaculate as any yacht. Superstructures glistened in the sun from their white-enamel coatings; and the masts, king-posts, and twin funnels, in various colours, added contrast. Winches and deck encumbrances had been thoroughly overhauled and painted. Lifeboats and life-saving appliances had been serviced. We looked—and were—an efficient ship.

The factory spaces had been treated in a like way. All machinery and electrical equipment had been serviced, and the vast machine plant looked spick and span with coatings of contrasting enamels. Even the safety guards had been carefully replaced on the machinery! The Factory Inspector would find no flaws when he came round to investigate. And down on the tank-deck the old tank bosun had seen to it that his gang had done their share.

Only the secretarial staff were busy now. All through the homeward voyage they had worked far into the night hours to complete the vast amount of essential clerical work. Pay-sheets and statements for every member of the expedition had to be meticulously compiled. Whaling returns had to be got ready . . . and there were the requisitions for next season.

Finisterre, Ushant, Casquets, St Catherine's, Dungeness, Dover, Forelands. We left them all behind us—great milestones for the home-coming deep-water seaman. We were in the North Sea. We were home, or so it seemed.

As we slowly wended our way up the Tönsberg Fjord we decreased speed to allow the scores of small motor-boats, packed with the families and friends of our Norwegian crew, to keep pace with us. Tönsberg was on holiday. We were the first arrival from Antarctica. Other expeditions would follow, but we had blazed the trail. The whole population of the man-hungry town seemed to have turned out. The male of the species had returned. It must have been like the return of the Yankee whalers home during the latter part of the last century. Nothing like this can be seen anywhere else. Tönsberg would go gay to-night.

There was feverish activity as our Norwegian personnel tried to obtain quick clearance from the ship. There was signing off and customs clearance to be attended to, farewells to be said, and then the 'welcome home' greetings from their families waiting in the off-lying boats.

British consulate officials had the signing-off job under way within minutes of our arrival. Customs clearance took more time. A score of officials were inadequate to cope with the hundreds of sea-bags, chests, and grips. The

Customs men went meticulously through the baggage. One would have thought we came from the East instead of from Antarctica. Still, the job had to be done.

Within six hours of our arrival we had seen the last of the Norwegians—at least, till next season—and we were ready for the final leg of the voyage. Nobody noticed our departure; they were all too busy with their own affairs.

Across the North Sea, through the Pentland Firth, along the north part of Scotland, down through the Minches, Mull of Kintyre abeam, and we were soon at the Liverpool Bar light-vessel. We embarked our pilot and proceeded up-river.

There were no 'welcome home' scenes here. The dock was practically deserted as we warped our hulking great ship into dock, assisted by four tugs. A few wharfingers with a couldn't-care-less attitude nonchalantly watched our arrival. What if we had just come from Antarctica, from the edge of the world? At last a few officials made their appearance, a small fleet of buses came alongside to convey the men to the railway-stations, and we began signing off our British crew. A few coastal tankers desultorily moored alongside us, and we started pumping out our whale-oil cargo.

And so another two hundred and more of our whalemen said their farewells. Only a skeleton crew remained.

That evening a few of us remained on board the now silent ship, tending the pumps and organizing the discharge of the cargo we had so strenuously earned. Only the cargo pumps made a noise now.

After a few drinks the talk always reverted to whales and whaling matters, to the whaleships and the men who manned them. And what of the whales—these great warm-blooded animals? Will they, like the bison of the plains of North America, be exterminated? Only a few thousand bison survive to-day, specially cared for in national parks—a grim and pathetic reminder of man's handiwork. Time will tell. After all, what is a hundred, a thousand years? It is but a few moments in the evolution of marine life.

The problem was too big for us. Anyway, who cared now? Soon we would be back on Tyneside. . . .

Index